Philosophical Perspectives

Max Scheler (1874-1928) was a leading figure in European philosophy during his generation. He was a collaborator and disciple of Husserl, founder of the phenomenological school of philosophy. Scheler's major work is a volume on ethics, *Der Formalismus in der Ethik und die materiale Wertethik*. Among his other writings are a sociology of knowledge, a sociology of religion, and works on philosophical anthropology. Of these latter works, *The Place of Man in the Universe* presents in sum the main points of his philosophical anthropology; it will soon be published by the Beacon Press.

Philosophical Perspectives

Max Scheler

Translated from the German by Oscar A. Haac

Beacon Press   Beacon Hill   Boston

104
5544p

Contents

Translator's Note

In order to conform to Scheler's intent, I have rendered his concepts by definite, specific terms and have attached more importance to this uniformity than to euphony, which dictated some of the interpretations of Peter Heath in his translation of Scheler, *The Nature of Sympathy* (London, 1954), cf. p. liii. I have consistently translated *"Geist"* as "spirit," not "mind," *"Bildung"* as "culture," not "education." Most important of all, I have adopted a standardized vocabulary to designate the three levels of knowledge and reality which Scheler established in order to integrate experimental science and relative phenomena into a metaphysical system, in order to find, as it were, the universal basis of a changing world:

(1) Sphere of concrete reality. The fortuitous existence of objects (*"das zufällige Dasein der Dinge"*) concerns the world of nature which is subdivided into inorganic (*"tot"*) nature and the organic, vital, or vitalistic (*"vitalistisch"*) realm of life, even though Scheler repeatedly protests against philosophers who establish dichotomies, such as of body and soul. All facts pertinent to this sphere are subject to analysis by experimental science (*"positive Wissenschaft"*) which represents man's monumental effort to control his environment and leads to knowledge of control (*"Herrschaftswissen"*), of work (*"Arbeitswissen"*), and of achievement (*"Leistungswissen"*). This kind of knowledge investigates the circumstance (*"Sosein"*) of things here and now, and grasps their continued existence (*"Dasein"*).

(2) Sphere of essence. A distinctly deeper level of understanding is accessible to man's noetic (*"noetisch"*) functions which, while pertaining to the actual human spirit (*"Geist"*), apprehend more stable realities than those of fortuitous existence and lead to knowledge of essence (*"Wesenswissen"*) or of culture (*"Bildungswissen"*), for culture (*"Bildung"*), as opposed to education (*"Erziehung"*),

concerns itself with fundamental, spiritual realities and universal forms (*"Gestalten, Formen"*) rather than with their particular manifestations. As opposed to the realms of *"Dasein"* (level 1) and *"Sein"* (level 3), this sphere concerns the nature (*"Wesen"*) of things, their essence.

(3) Sphere of metaphysical reality. By perceiving essences, man sees a reflection of absolute being (*"Sein"*) which emanates from the unchanging and ultimate source of all things (*"der Grund aller Dinge, Urgrund"*), Scheler's concept of God and divinity. This level of knowledge is described as knowledge of salvation (*"Erlösungswissen"*) and of grace (*"Heilswissen"*), i.e., of metaphysical reality (*"metaphysische Wirklichkeit"*).

I have clearly distinguished between what is (level 3) and what exists (level 1), and the terms "essential" (level 2) and "vital" (level 1) are never synonyms of "important," but refer to specific aspects of existence (level 1) and essence (level 2).

I have retained Scheler's parentheses, italics and quotation marks, also his distinction between technological civilization (*"Zivilisation"*) and spiritual culture (*"Kultur"*). It is useful to note that the terms "romantic," "literature," "literary" are always pejorative in Scheler and refer to dangerous figments of the imagination.

OSCAR A. HAAC

Emory University
Georgia

Philosophical Perspectives

I Philosopher's Outlook

"The masses will never be philosophers." These words of Plato are also valid today. Most men derive their view of the world from a religious or some other *tradition* which they imbibe with their mother's milk. However, the man who strives for an outlook founded on philosophy must dare to stand on his *own* reason. He must tentatively doubt all inherited opinions and must accept nothing which he himself cannot *clearly see* and prove. Although philosophy belongs and aways did belong to an *elite* centered around the outstanding personality of a thinker, an outlook founded on philosophy is by no means without influence on the course of history. For all history is essentially the work of elites and of those who imitate them. To find an example of the influence of a philosophical elite, one need but think of the influence of Plato and Aristotle on church doctrine, or of the powerful, moving, and inspiring effect of Immanuel Kant, Johann Gottlieb Fichte, Schelling, and Hegel on the Germany of the wars of liberation and on its political and military leaders, poets, and educators.

It is true that, until recently, German philosophy itself, especially its academic branch, did not try to develop a truly *philosophical outlook*. For decades, it exhausted itself trying to serve the experimental sciences as it tested their assumptions, methods, and aims. Thus, the philosophy of the last third of the nineteenth century dissolved almost exclusively into theories of knowledge and experience; yet, philosophy must no more be the mere servant of the sciences than the servant of religious faith.

In recent decades, philosophy has realized this and has fundamentally changed its nature and objectives. After long struggles it has again developed thorough and rigorous methods in order to bring

NOTE: First published in *Münchener Neueste Nachrichten* (May 5, 1928).

1

even so-called *"metaphysical"* problems closer to a solution, *in collaboration* with experimental science, but not under its patronage. Today, only a few stragglers continue the three major trends of thought, so-called positivism, Neo-Kantianism, and historicism, which declared that *all* forms of metaphysics were impossible. *Positivism* (e.g., Ernst Mach and Richard Avenarius) derived conceptions of being and knowledge from the evidence of sensory perception. It had to conclude that not only metaphysical solutions but even *investigations* of this kind were meaningless and based on false thinking "habits." So-called *Neo-Kantianism,* which, according to modern Kant studies, almost completely misunderstood the great thinker, did recognize metaphysical questions as eternal problems of reason, but considered them theoretically insoluble. *Historicism* (Karl Marx, Wilhelm Dilthey, Ernst Troeltsch, Oswald Spengler) saw in all views of the world, religious as well as philosophical, only changeable expressions of varying historical and social conditions. We can say today that philosophers have completely and fully refuted the reasons which these three groups of thinkers gave for their negative attitude toward metaphysics.[1]

It was necessary, however, not only to refute but to reconstruct in a positive spirit, and this was done. Man is not free to choose whether or not he wants to develop a metaphysical idea and a metaphysical awareness, i.e., an idea of the basis of man himself and of the world, of ontological reality which is only through itself (*ens per se*) and from which all other reality depends. Man, *necessarily* and always, consciously or unconsciously, *has* such an idea, such a feeling acquired by himself or inherited from tradition. All he can choose for himself is a good and reasonable or a poor and unreasonable idea of the absolute. Intellectual consciousness of absolute being is a part of man's *nature* and forms *a single* indestructible unit with consciousness of self, consciousness of the world, language, and conscience. Man can, of course, artificially exclude a clear consciousness of this realm by adhering to the sensory shell of the world. In such a case, the striving for the realm of the absolute persists, but the realm itself remains *empty* and without specific content. The place of the spiritual part of man also remains empty, and empty his heart. Even without being quite aware of it, man can fill this sphere of absolute being and of highest good with a *finite* content and good which, in his life, he treats "as if" it were absolute. Money, country, a loved one can be so treated. This is fetishism and idol worship. If man is to transcend this spiritual position, he must learn two things. First, through self-analysis, he must become conscious of the "idol" which, for him, has replaced absolute being and good. In the second place, he must smash this idol, i.e., put the overly loved object back into its *relative* position in the finite world. Then the sphere of the absolute will reappear, and only then will man be spiritually prepared to philosophize independently about the absolute.

Metaphysics is always *real*. This fact is only one reason why free philosophical investigation of the absolute is possible. Man, by right, also possesses the *means to know* and perceive the source of all things, cautiously and thoroughly, within limits that can be clearly determined, always imperfectly, but with truth and insight. He possesses, in the kernel of his individuality, the ability to win a *living share* in the source of all things. We shall show how he does this.

Man is capable of *threefold knowledge*—knowledge of *control* and achievement, knowledge of *essence* or culture, knowledge of *metaphysical reality* or salvation. None of these three kinds of knowledge exists for its own sake. Each kind serves to reshape a *realm of being*[2]—that of things, that of the culture pattern of *man* himself, or that of the *absolute*.

I

The first type of knowledge, that of achievement and control, serves our ability to exercise *power* over nature, society, and history. It is the knowledge of the *experimental specialized sciences* which support our entire occidental civilization. The supreme objective of this knowledge is to discover, wherever and in as far as possible, the *laws* regulating space and time relationships between environmental phenomena which can be definitely classified, the laws of their fortuitous circumstance here and now. We certainly do not seek such laws because we derive a special pleasure from laws, but for the sake of our *control* over the world and ourselves. Only what recurs according to laws can be predicted; only the predictable can be controlled. It is difficult to find such laws. Each day science discovers new ones and modifies old ones. In principle, however, it is always possible to find such laws. This is because sensory functions of all kinds (seeing, hearing, smelling, etc.), which we use for all possible *observations* and measurements, have been perfected by man, and by each animal, under the impetus and direction of their *drives* and *needs*. The lizard hears the softest rustle, but not the shot of the pistol. The control exercised by an organism can regulate only those elements and aspects of the actual world which recur in identical patterns according to the rule, "similar causes, similar effects." Therefore, our own and any *possible* sensory experience of animals is itself subject to an inner law. It tends to register *identical* rather than irregular segments of experience.

By analogy, physicists today wonder whether the ultimate and most fundamental laws of nature may not be just laws of a purely *statistical* type, laws of the "greatest number," and whether the principles involving *necessity,* in traditional physics, may not be solely the work of man. Space and time concepts, as Immanuel Kant correctly believed, do not stem from the content of our sensations but precede all sensory experience, like a plan and a diagram of all its potential individual patterns of content. Thus, even before space and time are conceptualized, e.g., visually or mentally represented, they are already inclusive terms for our capability to move spontaneously, inclusive terms for our capability to change spontaneously while doing and acting (time of eating, sleeping, space for motion). Only later on do we attribute to things *our* organic ability to move as *their* ability to move around each other. The same applies to time.

The inclusive terms for all potential movement and change, which space and time actually are, in the last analysis, serve only our desire to control reality. A purely intellectual being would have no reality, and *reality* is here the inclusive concept of *what resists our desires*.[2] Thus, one can imagine the magnitude of the error which, inherent in the natural outlook of man, held sciences under its spell for so long. This error consists in the assumption that space and time are infinite "empty forms" and that these would remain as inactive forms, by themselves, and, whether we existed or not, if things, matter, and energy were destroyed, that they are empty forms within which the finite world and the historical process are merely a strange "island." In a similar way, *all* the basic forms of being in our natural and experimental scientific conceptions of the world are *determined* not only by the nature of our reason, as Kant thought, but also and in addition by our active *drive for control over nature*.

II

The second type of possible knowledge is that of *the* fundamental philosophy which Aristotle called *"first philosophy,"* i.e., the knowledge of all forms of being and of the essential structure of all that is. It was not until relatively recently that Edmund Husserl and his school rediscovered that this *knowledge of essence* is a way of knowing sharply opposed to knowledge of control and to the realm of existence which corresponds to it. Knowledge of essence involves a tremendous field of philosophical investigation with its particular methods. Knowledge of control seeks, as we have seen, the laws of coincidence in space and time, laws of fortuitous realities in the world and of their circumstance. Conversely, the second direction of investigation rigorously and methodically *disregards* fortuitous place in space and time and what happens to be this way or some other way. Instead, it asks: *"What* is the world, what is, e.g., each so-called 'body,' each 'living being'; what is the *essence* of plant, animal, man, etc., in its invariable structure and essential qualities?" In a similar way it asks: "What is 'thought,' what is it to feel 'love' or 'beauty' quite independent from the fortuitous temporal stream of consciousness of this or that man in whom these activities *de facto* appear?"

What are the *main characteristics* of this kind of knowledge and investigation? First of all, the orientation toward controlling the world is replaced by the attempt to *exclude,* as far as possible, all attitudes based on the senses and *drives* since, as we saw, an attitude based on drives is prerequisite to all impressions of reality and also prerequisite to the formation of all sense perception of fortuitous *circumstance* here and now; prerequisite, also, to the preconception of space and time. Stated in positive terms, the orientation toward control, set on determining the laws of nature, consciously reflecting the *essence* of *what* is involved in the relationships subject to the laws of nature, is replaced by a *loving* attitude which seeks out the basic phenomena and ideas of the world.

In the second place, this orientation expressly disregards the real existence of things, i.e., their possible resistance to our desire and action, and thus disregards all simple fortuitous circumstance here and now such as that which sensory perception furnishes. We can, therefore, in principle, also gain knowledge of essence from things imagined. I am able, for instance, to see beyond movements on a movie screen or a good painting of a dog and to grasp, in addition, the ultimate components which pertain to the essence (*essentia*) of motion and to every "living being," etc.

In the third place, while knowledge of essence is not independent of all experience, it is independent of the *quantum* of experience or of so-called "induction." It precedes all induction just as it precedes all observation and measurement of reality. Such knowledge of essence can be derived from *each individual* case and example. *Once* such knowledge of essence, e.g., of the essence of life, has been acquired, it is valid "a priori," as schoolmen put it, i.e., "from the start," infinitely and generally valid, for all fortuitous observable facts concerning the particular essence, much as are principles of pure mathematics which render the multiple aspects of all *possible* natural phenomena and their inherent and necessary ideal relationships *before* real nature is explored by observation and measurement.

In the fourth place, it is precisely in this way that knowledge of essence and of essential relationships is valid, *above and beyond* that diminutive realm of the real world which is accessible to us through sensory experience and through any instrumental measurement which might support it. This knowledge is valid also for being *by itself and in itself*. It has a "transcendental" dimension, and thus becomes the jumping-off point for all "critical metaphysics."

Furthermore (in the fifth place), knowledge of essence in "first philosophy" is the true knowledge of *"reason,"* to be sharply distinguished from those extensions of our knowledge beyond sensory experience which rest solely on the mediate conclusions of the *"mind."* "Mind" or "intellect" enables an organism to adapt meaningfully to new situations for which the inborn instinct and associative memory have not prepared it. This happens suddenly and without reference to the number of previous trial attempts to solve the task.[3] This ability belongs not only to man but, to a lesser extent, also to animals, e.g., to the monkey who suddenly uses a stick to extend his reach in order to pull a fruit toward him. However, as long as the logical mind serves exclusively vital drives—the drives of food, sex, and power—and merely directs practical adjustment to stimuli of the environment, it is not yet specifically *human*. It becomes something specifically human only when the intellect (in animals there is only cleverness and cunning) begins to serve *reason*, i.e., applies formerly acquired, a priori knowledge of *essence* to the fortuitous circumstances of experience, when it, furthermore, begins to serve the highest insights into the relationships of the objective order of *values*, i.e., begins to serve *wisdom* and a moral idea.

Finally, knowledge of essence *can be applied in two ways*. It circumscribes the ultimate assumptions of the particular research of each field of experimental science (mathematics, physics, biology, psychology, etc.). Knowledge of essence furnishes each field the "axioms of its essential nature." In *metaphysics,* this knowledge of essence is what Hegel once very graphically called "the window into the absolute." For everything of *essential* nature, i.e., every truly basic phenomenon and idea, in the world and in the operations through which man plans and grasps his world, all that remains constant if one disregards the fortuitous distribution of things and acts in space and time—all this sets an insuperable limit for experimental science. Neither true essence nor the existence of something containing true essence can ever be explained or made intelligible by experimental science. The success of the task of experimental science depends precisely on strictly intentional exclusion of questions concerning the essence of things (e.g., *what* is life?). Therefore, both the essential structure and the existence of the world must, in the last analysis, be derived from *absolute reality,* i.e., from the common and supreme source of the world and of man's self.

The supreme aim in forming a metaphysical outlook through philosophy is, therefore, to conceive and consider absolute being through itself *in such a way* that it corresponds and is appropriate to the *essential* structure of the world as discovered in "first philosophy," to the real *existence* of the world as it appears to us in its resistance to our drives, and to all fortuitous circumstance.

From what we have already said we can establish *two fundamental attributes* of ultimate being. Ultimate being must contain an infinite, ideating *spirit* and a *rational power* which causes the essential structures of the world and of man himself to emanate jointly from itself. In the second place, it must contain an irrational driving force which posits equally irrational existence and fortuitous circumstance (the "images" we see), a dynamic, imaginative potency, the common root for centers and fields of force of organic nature and for the *one life* which rhythmically appears in the birth and death of all individuals and species. The philosophy devoted to inorganic and organic nature must show more precisely how this takes place. An increasing *understanding* of these two attributes of the activity of ultimate being thus forms the *meaning* of that historical phenomenon in time which we call "the world." The understanding is twofold. It is a *growing spiritualization* of the creative *driving force* which had originally been blind to ideas and ultimate values. From the other point of view, it is the *progressive acquisition of power and strength* by the infinite *spirit* which originally was powerless and could not formulate ideas. This process is most apparent in human history, where ideas and moral values slowly acquire a certain amount of effective "power" as they amalgamate more and more with interests and passions and with all the institutions resting on them.[4]

III

With these considerations, we have already reached the nucleus of the *third* type of knowledge accessible to man, the knowledge of *metaphysical reality* and *salvation.* "First philosophy," i.e., the ontology of the nature of the world and the self, is a springboard to this knowledge, but it is not yet metaphysics. We obtain *metaphysics* only when we tie *together* the findings of reality-conscious, experimental sciences and the results of ontological first philosophy and then relate both of these to the conclusions of the disciplines which involve judgment (general theory of values, esthetics, ethics, philosophy of civilization). This process leads us first to metaphysical "problems on the frontiers" of the experimental sciences, i.e., to metaphysics of the first order (what is "life," what is "matter"?) and, through it, to metaphysics of the absolute, metaphysics of the second order.

Between the metaphysical problems along the frontiers of mathematics, physics, biology, psychology, law, history, etc., and metaphysics of the absolute, there lies, however, one more important discipline which is now attracting interest and gaining significance, *"philosophical anthropology."* It asks *the* question in which Immanuel Kant (*Logic*) once said *all* philosophical problems meet: *"What is man?"*

All Western metaphysics before Kant had attempted to proceed from the being of the *cosmos,* or, in any case, from *concrete* being, to absolute, ontological being. This is what Kant, in his critique of reason (transcendental dialectics) proved to be *impossible.* Quite correctly, he stated that *all* concrete being, of the inner as well as of the outer world, must first be related to *man.* All forms of being depend on man's being. The concrete world and its modes of being are not "being in itself" but only an appropriate counterbalance to the entire spiritual and physical order of man and a "segment" of being in itself. A *conclusion* as to the true attributes of the *ultimate source* of all things can only be drawn by *starting from* the picture of the essence of *man* explored by "philosophical anthropology." This conclusion is an inverse prolongation of the spiritual acts which originally sprang from the center of man.

This way of reasoning and concluding is as important a (second) springboard toward modern metaphysics as "knowledge of essence." We call it the *"transcendental argument."* Its principle is: It is certain that the being of the world itself depends neither on the fortuitous existence of man on earth nor on his empirical consciousness. However, there are strong *essential analogies* between certain categories of spiritual *acts* and certain realms of *being* to which these categories give us access. For these two reasons, *all* acts and operations that grant this access to us transitory creatures *must* be ascribed to the source of all things. In other words, what shall we do if we can, e.g., prove that what space is accessible to us depends on certain motives of human action, but, nevertheless, must admit that a world of organized space was already present before the appearance of diluvial man? What are we to do if we must distinguish the absolute order of values itself from the changeable human view of the order of values, even though we must admit that an absolute order of values without a loving spirit realized in man is a contradiction in itself? By analogy, is not an order of ideas independent from us, without a thinker, as absurd as a reality without a "drive" to posit it? We can only relate the realms of being, which are and persist independently of short-lived man, to the acts of a single supra-individual spirit which must be an attribute of original being, is active in man, and *grows* through him. The same considerations apply wherever we find this *simultaneous* dependence and independence of things from earthly man. We can also say man is a microcosm, i.e., "a miniature world," because all essential aspects of being—physical, chemical, living, spiritual—are found in and intersect in man. Thus, the ultimate source of the "great world," the macrocosm, can also be studied in man. And for this reason the *being of man as microtheos is also the primary access to God.*

This modern metaphysics is no longer cosmology and metaphysics of concrete objects, but *metanthropology* and metaphysics of *action.* Its guiding principle is that the ultimate source of all which can concretely exist *cannot* itself be concrete but is, rather, a purely potential *actuality,* as the attribute of being which perpetually re-creates itself. The only access to God is, therefore, not theoretical contemplation which tends to represent God as a concrete being, but personal and active *commitment* of man to God and to *progressive* self-realization. It is a *collaboration* in the two attributes of the eternal act, in its spiritual power to create ideas as well as in its momentous force which we can feel present in our drives. The purest and supreme finite representation of both attributes is "man" himself. This kind of metaphysics considers it idolatry to make God into an object, a thing. Participation in the divine is possible only if one lives, plans, wills, thinks, and loves "in him" and through him and, so to say, *out of him.* Saint Augustine called it *cognoscere in lumine Dei, velle in Deo* [to know in the light of God, to want in God]. This completely excludes the material orientation which we usually find wherever the world, the self, and others are observed.

The spiritual *"person"* of man is neither a substantial thing nor a form of concrete entity. Man can rejoin his spiritual person only by acting. For this person is a hierarchical organic unit of spiritual acts which, at any moment, represents the unique and individual self-concentration of an infinite *spirit, one* and always the same, the root of the essential structure of the *objective world*. However, as a creature of drives and life, man is, by analogy, just as fundamentally rooted in the divine drive of *"nature,"* in the other attribute of God. This common root of all men and all life in the divine drive is sensed in the great movement of sympathy and love and whenever we feel one with the universe. This is the "Dionysian" way to God.

Man is thus not the imitator of a "world of ideas" or "providence" which arose spontaneously, or was already present in God before the creation, but he is *co*-creator, *co*-founder, *co*-executor of a stream of ideas which *develop* throughout world history and with man. Man is the only locus in which and through which original being grasps and recognizes itself, but man is also the being in whose free *decision* God can *realize* and sanctify his pure essence. It is man's destiny to be more than a "serf" and obedient servant, more also than merely the "child" of a ready-made and completed God. In his being as man, a condition involving *decisions,* man bears the higher dignity of an ally and even collaborator of God. Amid the storms of the world, man must carry before everything the flag of divinity, the flag of the *"Deitas"* [divinity] which realizes itself only *in the course of* world history.

Since the individual person of each man is *immediately* rooted in eternal being and spirit, no philosophical outlook is universally true, but, in each case, its "content" is valid only for one individual and history then determines its measure of perfection and appropriateness. There is, however, a universally valid *method* by which each person, whoever he may be, can find *"his"* metaphysical truth.

We have attempted, in these reflections, to indicate this method.[5]

II The Forms of Knowledge and Culture

The administration of this Cultural Institute, which has developed so remarkably in recent years under the patronage and inspiration of the genius of *Lessing,* has requested that I use the limited time available during this ceremony to say a few words about "knowledge and culture." A short time ago, I examined the problems at hand in detail, philosophically and scientifically, in two more extensive discussions entitled "The University and Popular Institutes" and "Problems of a Sociology of Knowledge." In the first of these, I demanded that we establish a new type of national free institute of culture on the highest educational level for the permanently employed who have passed normal student age. In honoring the request to speak here, I cannot present such well-developed arguments. It will have to suffice if I indicate, in short and concentrated sentences, at least a few of the convictions which I have reached in my research and through my experiences in teaching and life. They are, no doubt, significant for the objectives of a cultural institute.

Before everything I shall have to say as a philosopher, let me describe an almost painful impression which our times make on me, the impression of our period with its puzzling shallowness. I know of no time in history when the guiding elites were in greater need of true culture and when it was harder to attain. This tragic statement applies to our whole world, since it applies to our entire epoch, our age of disunity and of masses which are no longer controllable. But let me add: In our country, in Germany, the contrast between our needs and the difficulty of realizing these needs is relatively *very* great. We are a virgin forest in which the unity of national culture has been almost lost. I am not and am not known as a man who bluntly desires enlightenment, and even less as a partisan of what

NOTE: Address to the Lessing Institute, Berlin, January 17, 1925.

positivism calls "progress," but I find no other words than these:
One is seriously frightened because not only this or that country but
almost our entire civilized world is in grave danger of slowly and
almost inaudibly sinking and drowning in the gray, shapeless dawn
of non-freedom and hollowness which increases daily. And yet, *freedom* is the live, personal *spontaneity* of the spiritual center of man,
of man in man, and the most fundamental and first condition of our
ability to form and enlighten humanity.

Let us look around a little on the globe. Russia: An *"index
librorum prohibitorum"* [index of forbidden books], imitated from
the medieval Roman church, lists both Testaments, the Koran, the
Talmud, and all philosophers from Thales to Fichte. No book in
which the word "God" appears may pass the frontier. Following the
threadbare Marxist and pragmatic theories of the relationship between science and the national economy, Russia admits only those
contributions to knowledge which are of immediate use to technology,
hygiene, or economics. Marxism, today more drastically deranged
than ever before, has now been formally raised to the status of the
dogma of a large state. Tolstoy's late writings were solemnly burned.
North America and the United States as a contrast: There we find
a movement which calls itself "fundamentalism" because it wants to
make the Bible, in its literal interpretation, the absolute "foundation"
of knowledge and life. Based on this idea, there is a fast-growing
mass movement which asks nothing less than to have the government
prohibit teaching of and research in all forms of evolution (Lamarck-
ism, Darwinism, Vitalism) in the public schools. We also find a system of universities, which, in so far as it relies on contributions from
business, is degraded by its dependence on donors, be they petroleum
or gas interests or those of one or another bank. Upton Sinclair may
have exaggerated many things in *The Goose-Step*, a book worth
reading, but he has, no doubt, characterized the basic constitution
of this complex of culture, education, and research. In Italy: A
popular movement, "Fascism," with its cheap, childish, so-called
activism and vitalism. It cultivates a verbose and hollow philosophy

of history of the literary kind, imposed from above, which systematically spreads incense over Italian history but lacks all real links with the great tradition of a true philosophy which is more than "literature," or with the tradition of experimental science. Instead, for purely traditional reasons, its leaders execute empty and impious reverences before the Roman church. This means that they respect the Church of Rome, not as a venerable institution, guardian of universal truth and salvation, but merely as an element in Italian history and as the home of Dante, following the model of Maurice Barrès who said: "Je suis athée, mais je suis catholique" [I am an atheist, but I am Catholic]. In Spain: One of the noblest and most truthful minds, Unamuno, is exiled. The universities are fighting a vigorous battle for their existence against an overbearing clericalism.

The noble and free universities of Germany, seriously devoted to their fields of research, have, up to now, shown an encouraging and hardheaded resistance to so-called "popular movements" and their ideologies. Still, we must consider the strange phenomenon of a revolution which, contrary to the patterns of all true revolutions in modern times, has considerably strengthened the power of the Roman church. Thus we have in our day the Bavarian concordat imposing new obligations on schools and even universities, and we expect similar agreements in Prussia also.[1] An unworthy yearning for submission, salvation, protection of the soul in a beautiful, stylized system, a "shell," as Karl Jaspers correctly calls it, has seized considerable segments of our youth which is otherwise not lacking in noble qualities. The Neo-Catholic movement hardly asks whether this shell is *true* and *appropriate to reality*. It is as if, during an earthquake, everyone wanted to take refuge in the house which, in Europe, had longest resisted the ravages of time and which had demonstrated the greatest immunity to the movements of the ground. Everyone rushes and runs in that direction, not in order to cultivate his soul, not to seek *the* culture which corresponds to his own individual nature and destiny and to an objective, serious knowledge of contemporary culture, but in order to look for something quite different—a master who will direct how we are to think, act, and live. Even outside this movement we hear the constant call for "leaders." Might it not be the dawn of the era which Herbert Spencer predicted on his deathbed: "Socialism has to come and will come, but it will be the greatest misfortune humanity has ever witnessed. There will be no one left to act as he will, but everyone will have to do as he is told." I admit, the danger of inroads into the German universities is still small—of inroads into their old liberties which the power of our parliamentary parties directly invites, as does the authority of party leaders. Unfortunately, these leaders cannot, even partially, be identified with the elites of German culture. This fact is probably not based on personal, avoidable, or fortuitous reasons, but on historical reasons, deeply imbedded in the development of the new Germany and in its inherent *contrast between power and spirit*. We already have, of course, in Prussia and elsewhere, a few Marxist professors and the so-called "professors of Catholic ideology" in the universities without Catholic theological faculties. Their presence is quite contrary to the spirit of the German university. However, on the whole, the parties and their leaders have, up to now, treated freedom of research with encouraging respect. Fearfully one wishes: May it so remain!

If one surveys the entire mass of facts from which I have selected but a few illustrations, one can draw one conclusion. The noble forces of reason, philosophy, and science have risen throughout European history because of the progressive liberation of human activity from all forms of compulsion. They rose in close association, even shoulder to shoulder, with *democracy*. While this is undoubtedly true, the association has become a thoroughly "dubious" one for experimental science and so much the more for the philosophic disciplines which make up our true *"knowledge of culture."* We are facing the horrible *degradation of life to mass psychology*, the gradual transformation of a democracy of liberal ideas into a sullen democracy of masses, interests, and sentimentality, intensified by extending the voting privilege to women and to those only half mature. The leaders of this development are only the unoriginal mouthpieces of dominant group instincts, whether racial, ecclesiastic, or communistic. This condition is *one* important reason why "culture" is so hard to achieve today and why we absolutely must employ new, truly cultured elites who will forcefully resist this trend. It was not always democracy that furthered culture and knowledge in history. Think of Socrates and Anaxagoras! Think of the development of modern Japan which became a world power only through a kind of enlightened despotism. With the help of a small, *highly educated elite,* the emperor had to carry out all sensible reforms, from the introduction of stone houses to that of science, in opposition to the democracy of his country, which was steeped in sullen tradition and bias and opposed to all modern ideas. Today, democracy has only *one* means of saving itself from dictatorship and of salvaging cultural and scientific values. It must restrain itself and *serve* spirit and culture without wanting to dominate them. Otherwise, there would be only one solution—an enlightened dictatorship which pays no attention to the anticultural masses and to its leaders, but rules them with the whip, the saber, and sugar plums.

If we briefly examine the philosophical movements of our time and their relationship to true culture and knowledge, we discover many deeply disturbing elements in the total picture, in spite of the admirable accomplishments of science, especially in the natural sciences. In my essay on the sociology of knowledge, cited above, I have emphasized that the theory and sociology of knowledge in our society increasingly approach the structure of the Alexandrine-Hellenistic age. Then, as today, the unity and noble order of Greek and Roman culture was being progressively replaced by ever new associations, circles, crudely mystical and superstitious sects, questionable saviors who were experts in mass psychology, and, at the opposite extreme, by a technological (Alexandrine) positivism devoid of ideas. In that essay, I further singled out the following movements in present-day Germany and explained in detail why they are harmful for true philosophy and science: First, the false elevation of the Marxist class ideology of the proletariat to a supposed special "science," a "proletarian science," which is opposed to "bourgeois" science as if science (as distinguished from "ideology") could ever be the function of a class. Second, the mistaken forms of gnostic neo-romanticism, which reduce our powerful culture of specialized sciences into a presumptuous and spurious sham of a philosophy and, in turn, reduce philosophy to mysticism and a too facile intuition (Bergson, the circle around George, Von Kahler). Third, the scholastic theologies which increasingly penetrate philosophy and science. They think in terms of an epoch and a society dead for four centuries. Fourth, the "anthroposophic," antiphilosophical, and anti-scientific nature of a large part of the occult movements. Fifth, the dim ideologies of racist mass movements, ignorant of European reality and drunk with imaginary, absolute race theories which darken our international horizons in every way. They are unaware that the world situation demands a new solidarity of European nations. Sixth, the presumptions of egocentric medicine men of all kinds, ridiculously conceited, painful dillettantes, less and less critical as their sub-missive following grows. All this is decline and decadence.[2]

This Institute bears the noble name of *Lessing,* the name of the man who combines science, wisdom, grace, and spirit with the noble, clear reputation of an upright, daring personality and with a chivalrous sword of finest, hardest steel, something which German scholars and intellectuals unfortunately possess only rarely. This Institute should, therefore, consider that its *first* task is to reconquer as much as possible of our *free right to culture* which we are in danger of losing if present trends persist.

But enough of this and of our times! The solemn hour demands that we do more than dwell on these difficult and dark problems. In these times, when a *new kind of man* is trying to take shape in the painful struggle for a new world, the center of interest is the *cultural development of man.* Yet, a *philosophical definition of culture* has seldom been attempted.

Whoever would *attain culture* or *impart it to others,* if this can be accomplished by an outsider, needs clear insight into three problems: First, what is the *essence* of "culture"? Second, *how* does culture *arise?* And third, what types and what *forms of knowing* and knowledge condition and determine the process through which man becomes "cultivated"?

If we consider "culture," *cultura animi* [the culture of the spirit], not as a development but as something perfect, we find it to be primarily a form, a shape, and a rhythm peculiar to each individual. It delimits and orders all free activities of the human spirit. It also guides and directs all psychophysical and automatic aspects of life (expression and action, speech and silence), the entire "comportment" of man. *Culture is therefore a category of being,* not of knowledge and experience. Culture is the result of molding, of shaping this *total* being of man. It is not the kind of molding and shaping of a material substance which takes place when a statue is formed, but that of a living entity within the order of *time,* a unity which consists only of developments, processes, and acts. This cultural being of the person corresponds, in each case, to *one* specific world, to a "microcosm," an entity in itself. Each of its parts and segments concretely illuminates the molded, life-evolved form of this and no other individual, with more or less intense light, like an objective reflection. This microcosm is not a limited *area* of the world. It is neither an object of human knowledge and culture nor a force resisting man's efforts and action. It is a world *entity* in which all essential ideas and values find themselves reproduced and organized into structural order, *all* of them realized in one great, absolute, and real universe and in a fortuitous existence which man never fully grasps. One such "universe," summed up and encompassed in *one* particular human being, is the *world* of culture. In this context, Plato, Dante, Goethe, Kant each have *their* "world." We men cannot fully grasp particular fortuitous objects except through an infinite series of experiences and observations, but we can comprehend the *essential* structure of the entire world.

"The human soul, in a certain sense, is—everything." This is the famous proposition of Aristotle. It inspired the idea of "microcosm" as it was being interpreted from Thomas Aquinas, Nicolaus de Cusa, Giordano Bruno to Leibnitz and Goethe. According to this idea, the world-segment, man, and the whole of the world are differentiated in their fortuitous existence, but they are *identical in essence,* and the whole of the world is *fully* contained in man as part of the world. The essences of *all* things intersect in man and find solidarity in man. Thomas Aquinas says: *"Homo est quodammodo omnia"* [in some way man is all things].[3] "To strive for culture" means to try, with loving fervor, to participate ontologically and take part in all aspects of nature and history which are *essential* to the world, and not just fortuitous existence and circumstance. This implies the desire to be a microcosm like Goethe's Faust. Such concentration of the world at large, of the "macrocosm," into the particular spiritual center of *one* individual, the "microcosm," or such expansion of one human being who, in love and insight, grows into a *world*—these are merely two inverse manifestations *of the same* fundamental creative development which we call culture. The world has evolved *realiter* [really] until it found expression in man, and man should evolve *idealiter* [ideally] until he becomes a world!

The fountainhead of this process is man's love for the world. It is not "Platonic" love in the common acceptance of the term, but indeed the love of the *true* Plato, ever and insatiably thirsting for poetic reunion and sympathy with all aspects of world essence. It is the love which, once upon a time, permanently bestowed its name on all *"philosophia"* as *love for essence.* To grasp this Eros conceptually has been the ever-renewed ambition shared by Plato, Aristotle (in his concepts ὀρέγεσθαι [to reach out for God], ἐφίεσθαι [to lose oneself in God]), Giordano Bruno ("heroic love"), Spinoza *("amor Dei intellectualis"* [intellectual love of God]), Leibnitz, Goethe, Schelling, Schopenhauer, Eduard von Hartmann, and myself. It is a strange love—a love which is passionate thirst *and, at the same time,* supreme *objectivity* in assessing concrete values. It is indeed the root of all "objective" attitudes. Without eliminating the eternal order of essential values, this love, in its ultimate goodness, *accepts* everything which mysteriously arose from nothing, tolerates everything one can neither praise nor admire, and calmly blesses even the circumstances that bring suffering. It is, therefore, characteristic of culture not to despise anything altogether, always to feel safe deep in one's soul, and to be "composed." It is the spirit *"nil humani a me alienum puto"* [I consider nothing human foreign to me], the spirit of Schiller's fleet-footed verse: *"Calmly,* supported by the graces and muses, he receives the menacing arrow . . . from the *gentle* bow of necessity."

To this first definition of the essence of culture, arising from the idea of the microcosm, let us add the following: *Culture is* both *the growth to become man* as seen from the level of subhuman nature *and, simultaneously,* as part of the same process, the continuous attempt of *"self-deification"* as seen by all superhuman and infinite things which exist and are and demand our veneration.

We know that thing we call "man" still quite insufficiently. From the background of the natural sciences, one is justified in defending the proposition that he is an animal which has fallen sick or which remained behind its most closely related companions in organic adaptation and especially in capacity to adapt.[4] Looking at man purely as a creature of nature and viewing him objectively, his most obvious anatomical trait is the unusually developed, differentiated, and hierarchical structure of his nervous system, especially of the cortex. This organ, *diametrically* opposed in every respect to the organs and functions of reproduction, is most essential to the entire organism because it regulates the imposing and releasing of controls over instinctive behavior. A certain though relatively small number of these functions of the cortex are surely connected with the psychic life functions capable of producing consciousness. Man shares some of these with the highest vertebrates, but others have become *peculiarly his own,* since he phylogenetically developed new segments of the brain not present in animals (e.g., the cerebrum, so important for his upright walk and his span of attention). Numerous contemporary investigations have established that particular achievements and psychic functions, in the development of the species as well as of individual beings from childhood to puberty, maturity, and old age and death, directly correspond to the developmental stages of the brain and to the nature of its physiological function. We are facing more than a simple "parallel" between psyche and physiology, as might result from simply observing two different species of the same psychophysical, indifferently rhythmical pattern of life, i.e., from observing the individual being as it sees itself, is for itself, and seems and appears to others. Instead, we are facing a case of *functional identity* of psyche and physiology.[5] Though individual movements may originate either in the channel of consciousness or through physical or chemical stimuli, we find here *one single life, one identical rhythm,* irreducible to a mechanism, though manifest in different ways, in the experience of the self and others, in observation of the external and the inner world. The processes of this rhythm unfold in a peculiar *teleoclinic* way, according to their own principles, in their peculiar periodicity. They always follow strictly analogous principles which relate them to the *whole,* i.e., to an indivisible *totality* which includes maintenance and growth, but also the decline and death of the psychophysical organism.

Living beings are thus distinguished by a series of largely anatomical differences. Like all structural forms of live organic matter, they must, in the last analysis, be understood *in terms of their functions,* i.e., as individually different, relatively stable, functional patterns of chemical and physical amalgams of matter and packets of energy. Far more important, however, than anatomical differences is the tremendous *physiological* gulf which separates man even from the highest vertebrates.[6] Advanced and thorough research of our day[7] has established exactly, and quantitatively, that man's brain consumes enormous quantities of energy derived from food, heat, etc., as compared with that of the next lower animal, and that it withdraws this energy from the other organs and functions of the body. If we compare the achievements of man with those of animals, all of which lack a cerebral cortex, man appears as the veritable *slave* of his cortex. Compared with all other organs of the body, the cortex is *least* able to recuperate, least capable of phylogenesis. Its vital force seems completely *petrified*. The cortex is normally responsible for natural death. Man, the most "cerebral" of creatures, combines the shortest history as a species with the relatively longest life-span of the individual. As a species, he is the most recent creature on earth. He is the most transient of all species or, in any case, came late in the evolution of life and (even if we assume no special imminent catastrophes) will most likely be the first species to die out.

These considerations are of exceptional philosophic significance. Eduard von Hartmann has already furnished a more solid basis for the theory that a species can originate as a result of true mutation and die out in a natural manner. The best recent investigations concerning this question[8] have corroborated this more and more. Thus, they contradict the theories of Weismann which long dominated biology. Even cell plasma *ages*. Eduard von Hartmann has added another important thesis. As living beings reach a higher stage of development, they generally *lose* their ability to develop as a species and become less likely to acquire new characteristics that effect more than adaptation and locale, i.e., the whole of morphology. Therefore, the species man is *least* likely to evolve. "Superman," in the biological sense, is a fairy tale. Even Weismann calls man the *most stable* of animal species. We know that, as nations rise in civilization and culture, their fertility rate declines. This phenomenon is closely accompanied by an increase in individualization and in the value attached to the individual life and being. All this is perhaps a (rather remote) consequence of the more general biological principle stated above. This consequence reflects the polar contrast between the functions of the brain and of reproduction.

In view of this and many similar facts, we have some justification for asking: Is not this *homo naturalis* man, as a biological being, a real *"dead-end road of nature,"* a kind of nature which has, so to speak, arrested its progress and lost its way in man, and which can advance no further by means of *those* methods which, in evolution, led to the creation of man? I can give only brief and approximate reasons for this. For, having lost his way, man seems to have become spirit and a "history" led and directed by the spirit. If we consider it *exclusively* from the point of view of natural science, we find that this history, with all its mighty doings and activity, with its most complex detours (via tool, technology, state, etc.), has accomplished *nothing* more than the evolution of animals. I mean that they have become *equally* proficient in maintaining the species and in realizing specifically biological values of all kinds! In fact, animals achieved these results much more simply and automatically through their instincts, self-training, and trial and error, and also through the "practical intelligence" which appears at the highest level of the animal kingdom in anthropoid apes. The expression, "practical intelligence," objectively designates here the ability to meet new, atypical situations in a biologically meaningful way, without second attempts or errors, and without need for practice.

This conception of the nature of man is irrefutable *only* from the background of natural science. It assumes that the element which European tradition, since the Greeks, has called "spirit" and "reason" is merely a complicated by-product of the dualistic life-process. Those who accept this position should be consistent and also *renounce* the idea and value of "culture." [9] For culture implies an *intrinsic value,* whereas the above definition can admit culture only as a "means" of maintaining and intensifying life. Ideas and intrinsic values and, above all, the *essential value* of the spiritual, rational person in man, outstripping all values of achievement and life, can and may be accepted only by those who see man as a citizen of *two* worlds, in the tradition of Kant and of all great European philosophers, or, better, by those who see man as a being rooted with the two different attributes of his essence in *one* source of the world which is divine substance. I mean those who can *distinguish* in each object the *essence* (what it is) from its fortuitous existence here and now, its circumstance; who can conceive of essence in the radiance of "spirit" and "reason," or, more poignantly, by becoming subjects solely determined by *purpose* and unassuming *love*. I mean those who see, in the radiance of such fundamental "spiritual" acts of man, a new manifestation of the *very* essence of the ultimate source of things which cannot be derived empirically or biologically; who understand that this ultimate source of things is even more than purposeful *force*, *instinct, and drive*, though these are basic to all inanimate and living nature, and basic also to man as a creature of nature and biological life;[10] for this source of the world is *itself* "spirit" and "reason," itself all-loving, all-perceiving, and all-thinking light.

As a vitalistic being, man is doubtless a dead-end road of nature, its end and simultaneously its greatest concentration. However, as a potential "spiritual being," as a potential manifestation of the divine *spirit itself*, as a being capable of *"deifying"* itself in its active collaboration with the spiritual acts of the source of the world, man is something quite distinct from a dead-end road; he is the clear and magnificent way to escape this dead-end road, the creature in which fundamental essence begins to know and grasp itself, to understand and save itself. Man is both a *dead-end road* and a *way of escape*.

This conception of the *essence* of man opposes him not only to the highest vertebrates, the anthropoid apes, but to *all of nature* as a creature that may smile down at nature since the *ultimate center of its being* is free from nature's driving forces. We take this conception of man to contain nothing of the *fortuitous* empirical characteristics of the creature on earth, living in our epoch and called by the same name;[11] we see here solely *"the vital being capable of spiritual acts."* Thus, man becomes the starting point of all relative, though perhaps unconscious, *deification*, when and wherever he is qualitatively *more* than the animal. So conceived, he is not a being at rest, a given fact, but only a possible *direction for development* and, simultaneously, an eternal *task* and an eternally resplendent objective for man as a living creature. In this context, man does not "exist" as an object, nor even as a relatively constant object, but only as constant *potential growth to the state of true humanity* which can be freely accomplished at any moment, a process of truly *becoming* man which, even in historical times, never subsides, although it is often accompanied by a tremendous retrograde movement—a relative return to animal status. At every moment of life this regress opposes the process of humanization in individuals and nations. What we have discussed is *simultaneously the idea* of *humanity* and the essence of classical and Christian *"deification."* This combined idea of humanization and deification is as inseparable from the idea of "culture" as is the concept of "microcosm," discussed earlier.

In spite of the clear, evident, and tremendous differences between the *accomplishments* of man and animal, hardly anyone has, up to now, fully recognized the functional complex of action and thought and its laws which explain the specific, *unique attributes* of *homo sapiens,* i.e., language, constant upright walk, religion, science, formed as a tool and applied "as such," conscience, capacity for artistic representation, ability to name objects, a feeling for justice, formation of states, development of concepts, historical progress, etc. The student of animal psychology who seeks to establish these human prerogatives, will experience, with ever renewed astonishment, what these words express: "It is *difficult* to be man. It is *rare,* very rare indeed, that the biological species, man, is man within the connotation of the idea of *humanitas* [true humanity]." I usually say to my students: "Learn to know animals so that you will know how *difficult* it is to be man."

The young science of animal psychology which progresses so vigorously possesses great value, even for philosophy, because it has shown how much people tended to *underestimate* the psychic qualities of animals. Thus, only a short time ago, animals were credited with hardly more than what is called associative memory, i.e., it was recognized that the tasks which the animal must solve cause repetitive reactions governed by the principles of association, and that the physiology of the organism, its physiological drives, as well as the conditions of its environment, determine these reactions. This suffices to explain that the animal can be trained by pleasure and pain, reward and punishment, and also that it can train itself by "trial and error," and that its behavior becomes gradually fixed through the accumulation of successful experience.[12] Furthermore, people attributed to the animal something expressed by the obscure word "instinct," i.e., an inborn and inherited ability to meet typical, repeated situations in a *meaningful* manner by a regular, rhythmical succession of attitudes *characteristic of the species,* as if the animal already knew the final result of its behavior without actually having it in front of its eyes, just as man has before his eyes the so-called "purpose" of his actions. As a part of the morphogenesis of the animal organism, this ability of animals did not require experience, learning, or habit, but needed only to be trained in specific directions. In instinct, desire and knowledge act as if they were still one and the same. Today we must say—we can say—in view of the results of research in animal psychology: The animal certainly possesses *more* than these two abilities, associative memory and instinct, even if it is difficult to assess exactly how much more. At least among the higher vertebrates, the animal manifests also the beginnings of "technical intelligence," as we defined it earlier, and, with it, the ability to *choose* meaningfully in a manner not rigidly typical or generically determined. Thus, it can also meet *new* situations, without trial and error, in a meaningful manner appropriate to the circumstances, and it can, to some extent, use objects as tools without, of course, always using the *same* object "as a tool," or without attributing to objects the permanent *designation* of tools. Truly altruistic actions of animals used to be denied, but they exist. They have been observed with certainty and go far beyond the instinct to care for the litter and the period of heat.

Formerly, the true dignity and significance of man was often not realized, precisely because the animal soul was *underestimated.* Practical, technical intelligence is not what makes man into true man, in the context of essential being, as people used to think; only the *quantity* of technical intelligence has increased tremendously in man, to the level of a Siemens or an Edison. The only new element not shared by animals is man's capacity to act *autonomously* in the face of all psychic, vital causality (including practical intelligence governed by drives), a causality no longer analogous and parallel to the functional processes of the nervous system, but parallel and analogous to the *objective structure of objects and values in the world itself*. The animal finds *in* objects the kind of psychic experience which, in man, could be called a momentary "ecstasy." A monkey that jumps about, instinctively attracted by one object, then by another, lives, so to speak, in a series of separate temporary ecstasies. Only man *sets himself* and his "consciousness of self" *apart* from the world. Only he separates concrete environment from his personal experience of self. Only he can perceive an object through his different senses and realize that it is "one and the same." The animal, it is true, is conscious of the general, but it cannot, at the same time, differentiate the general content and the individual object, grasp the relationships between the content of several general experiences, or grasp them and manipulate them independently, separate from concrete situations and instances where they can be applied. The animal does have the ability to prefer one *desirable good* to another, e.g., one food to another, a greater to a smaller amount of satisfaction. It can also choose that action, among several, which results in the attainment of what it prefers. Animals are not just "blind" creatures of drives, as people used to represent them. However, the animal *cannot*, abstractly, without reference and connection to specific, concrete *objects* which represent values, prefer one *value* to another which stands lower in the scale of values in the way man might prefer "the" useful to "the" agreeable, as such, or prefer to preserve and realize a spiritual value (honor, dignity, spiritual welfare, conviction) rather than preserve the highest value of physical life—his own existence.

There are, in the last analysis, *three basic conditions*[13] from which one can derive the true functions of the human spirit and reason which I have just illustrated: (1) The spiritual subject, man, can be determined only by the contents of the *object* and not by drives, physical needs, and inner conditions of the organism. (2) A *love* free of physical desire raises him above everything in his environment which is determined by drives. (3) He is able to distinguish what something is (being) from the way it happens to occur (existence). Essential being is revealed to him as he loses and severs his dependence on worldly drives and as he reduces the existential impressions which pertain to such dependence. Thus, he can derive valid insights which remain true for all fortuitous objects and all instances of the same essence ("a priori insight"). Therefore, anyone who denies a priori insight in man reduces him unwittingly to an animal.[14]

Without these three functions it is impossible to become *"conscious of the world,"* as opposed to merely *"possessing an environment"* as does the animal. In contrast to the values of physical life and its psychic functions, to which the animal is tied exclusively, one can designate the three human functions as those of a relative asceticism. Indeed, within the context of organic species, man is the *relative "ascetic of life."* This fully corresponds to the finish and dead-end of life which, as we have seen, he represents. Universal evolution, through which the divinity realizes its essence and reveals its ceaseless becoming, finds in man a realm of what is and has true value, a realm which *transcends all possible milieux of physical life* and stands enthroned *above* everything, important or unimportant, in merely vital context. Therefore, what we call "free will" in man, as opposed to drive and instinct, is *not* a *positive* power to produce and create, but a negative power to *control and release* the impulses of drives. The act of will, related to action, is always primarily a *"non fiat"* [it shall not be done] rather than a *"fiat"* [it shall be done].[15]

From the functions which I designated as primary acts of the spirit, one is by necessity driven to a *concept of the constitution of man.* Man is the being, intrinsically *lofty* and *noble,* raised above all of physical life and its values, even above all of nature, the being in which the psyche has *freed* itself from *subservience* to life and has purified itself into "spirit," a spirit in whose service "life" enters in an objective as well as in a subjective, psychic sense. We have here an ever new and growing process of "becoming man" in this specific sense, a humanization which is both self-deification and a collaboration in realizing the idea of divinity. It is not waiting for a savior from the exterior, nor receiving capitalized gifts of salvation through a church that worships its founder as a God in human likeness, nor salvation received for true and personal discipleship and action. It is, rather, *self*-deification, and that means also *collaboration* in realizing the idea of the *spiritual* divinity which is "essentially" present in the substrata of the life force. This life force, always identical, underlies all forms of natural life and all growth, impels all drives, and manifests itself in inanimate and live substance, following various principles, in those "images" we call "bodies." In such deification and collaboration I see the nucleus of culture, as well as the ultimate justification of its meaning and value.

Man, a brief holiday in the tremendous expanse of time, of universal growth of life, thus *means* something in the development of God *himself*. Man's history is not merely a spectacle for an eternal, perfect, and divine spectator and judge, but is interwoven into the growth of God himself.[16] There *is* a human animal which *evolves* and constantly renews his self-development into God and spirit-related manhood. Throughout "world" history, he continuously develops what is incipient in its *essence,* in the sense of Pindar who said: "Become the one you are." Through the active energy of all his drives (hunger, power, libido) and blood, he feeds the spirit that originally was impotent, that in its original form lacked any activity which could increase in intensity, and merely "was as a potential." He *realizes and embodies* this *spiritual idea,* which is his own, right into his fingertips and into the smile of his mouth. All this is not just a way to ascertain achievements, the so-called "cultural advance." It is not a mere by-product of history. Rather, all this is the *meaning of the earth, indeed, of the world itself*. This is an objective existing *only* for its own sake and for the sake of the divinity that, without man and his history, could not attain its own purpose and would not realize the aim of its own timeless development. Each historical activity culminates not in goods, artistic achievements, not in the unending extension of knowledge through the experimental sciences, but in this well and nobly created *being* of man, in his *collaboration in realizing God.* Not only the Sabbath exists for the sake of man's spiritual well-being *in Deo,* but all civilization, all culture, all history, even state, church, and society. *Salus animarum suprema lex* [the supreme law is the welfare of souls]. Culture is not "technical preparation for something," "for" a profession, field of specialty, or achievement of some kind. Culture does not exist *for* the sake of such preparation. Rather, all professional preparation "for a purpose" exists for the sake of culture which lacks all external "useful aims," for the sake of the *well-formed man himself.*[17]

But, and this is a most important but, one achieves certain objectives only if one does *not* plan them *willfully.* Values, like their subjective resonances, feelings, become less precious, the more directly and easily one can willfully plan and realize them, the more the blessings which sustain them must be shared in order to be generally available.[18] Culture is, of course, *"determination of purpose,"* individual and unique designation of cultural spheres, nations, and, ultimately, of each individual, but it is *not* a possible, direct *objective* of the will. Culture is *not* "a desire to make oneself into a work of art"; it is *not* egocentric self-planning, be it of one's own beauty, virtue, form, or knowledge. It is the exact opposite of this intent to enjoy oneself which culminates in "dandyism." Man *is* not a work of art and *should* not be one! The *growth* of culture happens and takes place behind the back of mere intent and mere will, while man's life unfolds *through* the world and *with* the world, as he acts, in love and deed, to overcome passions and obstacles in himself and in the world, whether they relate to environment, fellow-men, or the state, as he works hard, profits from his labor, increases, raises, and expands his *powers and the self,* ultimately wishing for true deification of the act, in the spirit *velle, amare in Deo* [wanting, loving in God],

of *cognoscere* in *lumine Dei* [knowing *in* the light of God], as Augustine and Luther designated this unconditional deification of the act.
Only the man willing to *lose* himself in a noble cause or in some kind
of true companionship, unafraid of what might be the outcome, will
win himself, that is his true self, will win it directly from the divinity,
out of the force and the purity of the divine breath.

What is the most effective and forceful external *stimulus* to
culture? What *outside* elements must supplement our orientation,
the unique and always individual value of our chosen direction which
we are destined to realize and which constantly keeps before our
eyes a true self love *"in Deo"* for the deepest essence of our own
being, which is the "idea" God has of us? What do we need to meet
actively the call of our *destiny,* the quiet demands of this ideal, so
overwhelming that we seem smaller the closer we approach it? Much
is needed, and only a small part of it is under our control! For
life is *daemonic,* in Goethe's sense, neither divine nor infernal, while
the mighty aspect of so-called "history," called *fate,* is playfully
indifferent in its tremendous determinism of heredity, milieu, condition of groups and classes, times, and a thousand other elements.

If we now look, not at these conditions which, by necessity, let
so many noble seeds be lost in darkness, but at positive stimuli to
culture, the first and foremost appears to be the *example of worth we
discover in a person* who has won our love and admiration. *At least
once* the *entire* man must have been submerged in something whole,
pure, free, and noble, if he wants to become "cultured." There are
also models who drive us to negative reaction. One should avoid
them! One does not "choose" such a model. One is captivated by it
because it seduces, invites, and attracts us imperceptibly. National
heroes, exemplary members of our profession, moral and artistic
models, finally, the rare example which this world has witnessed of
purest and highest human culture itself, the very small number of
saints, of pure and complete persons—these are our steppingstones
and also the trailmakers. They explain and clarify the individual's
own purpose. By their example we can measure our skill and strive

to attain our spiritual selves. They teach us to know our true *powers* and how to use them.

However, true culture necessarily *differentiates*. It is foolish to want to be like Goethe, Luther, or Kant (as our popular orators say), or like some jumble of so-called "great men." We should be more intent on giving the good and pure, the truly cultured, an opportunity of also becoming "great," i.e., *effective* in history, than on crawling before the so-called "great men" of history, who, all too often, became "great" only because of the wickedness and smallness of the men of their time.

Each individual, also each group, each profession, each period and its leaders, possesses *its own* special and characteristic pattern of drives, i.e., particular order of primary drives, and has *its own* peculiar spirit. Therefore it also has *its own special models*. Eduard Spranger, in his recent book, *Lebensformen,* was thus quite justified in demanding that cultural ideals be *differentiated* so as to conform to the disposition and talents which, in each person, mark the characteristic trends of growth to manhood and humanity. It was the grave error of the eighteenth century, fatal for the development of the humanistic ideal in the nineteenth, that it understood the cultural ideal of "humanity" only in the abstract form of a rational capacity *equal* in all men. Romanticism, with its yearning for authority and its worship of great men, merely represented a reaction, in part rather dissolute, against the one-sided, abstract, rationalistic idea of humanity. "Spirit," however, is individualized *in itself,* not only in its abstract existence, but in its *concrete circumstance.*[19] It is not individualized merely by the content of its fortuitous, external or internal experience, nor by its association with one physical person and his hereditary talents. The spiritual person in man is an *individual, unique self-concentration* of the divine spirit. For this reason, heroes do not require imitation or blind submission, as is so often advocated in our Germany that yearns for authority. Heroes are only precursors, enabling us to hear the calling of *our particular* person. They are the dawn in the sunny day of our *individual* conscience and principle.

These model personalities are to *free* us, and do free us, just as they themselves are free and not slaves. They leave us free to pursue our own calling and to fully exercise our powers. General laws are always merely negative laws, like the laws of nature and the principles of ethics. They say what shall *not* happen or perhaps what we must not do, rather than what we shall do or become. In addition, they are laws of averages, laws for the greatest number, which do not bind us unconditionally, but only conditionally.[20]

Eighteenth-century thinkers, Kant included, also erred in not noticing in history the common, real *growth of the spirit itself* and of what the technical language of philosophy calls "a priori" forms of thought, reflection, value judgment, preference, love, etc. They erred in assuming the historical constancy of rational forms and because they recognized only the accumulation of historical *achievements,* goods, works, on top of which each generation could stand as on a mountain. There is, however, also spiritual growth or, of course, spiritual decline, independent of biological and nervous changes in man. Recently I wrote: "Changes in the *forms* of thought and conception, as in the transition from a *'mentalité primitive'* (as recently described by Lévy-Bruhl) to the civilized state of human thought which thus begins to follow the principle of differentiation and individualization; changes in the forms of spirit which are forms of *value* judgment (not merely appraisal of possessions based on *one* individual order of values or 'spirit'); changes in feeling for style or general desire for art (as have been assumed since Riegl); changes from the early occidental, organological view of the world (which was held until the thirteenth century) to a mechanistic view; changes like those from a society of predominantly family clans, not subject to the authority of a state, to the epoch of 'political society' and of the state; or from a predominantly 'communal' society to modern 'social' organization; or from a predominantly magical science to experimental technology; all these transformations are of an entirely different *order* of magnitude (not changes in magnitude) than the following: Changes resulting from the cumulative *application* of a rational capacity which is already developed (as represented, for instance, by the Occidental form of logic); or transformations in the 'practical morality' and those involved when *one* spirit is adapted to changing historical conditions, e.g., when the Christian spirit was adapted to the economic and social conditions of late antiquity, the Middle Ages, or of modern times; or changes taking place only *within* a predominantly organological and mechanistic philosophical outlook." When sociology studies the development of knowledge, there is no distinction more important that this: Is there change in the *forms themselves* of thought, value judgment, and perception of the world, or only in their *application* to our environment, as our experience is *quantitatively* and *inductively* expanded? We must develop exact and precise theoretical criteria for this distinction.[21]

This leads me to the *process of cultivating the spirit and to the forms of knowledge* which serve this development. I want to indicate only what is most important, the underlying principle, and see by what kind of knowledge our spirit itself grows, how it becomes "culture." It is clear that it does not grow through its own achievements and works. In order to discover this, we must lay our finger on the hidden way in which specifically human knowledge, primary and objective *knowledge of the essence of things, becomes functional* or, we might say, *categorical.* Wherever this takes place we find, so to speak, a transmutation of objective knowledge into a new life force and function, a force which enables man to seek and perceive ever new objectives and to incorporate them into his knowledge, in a *form and manner* learned from the first act of knowledge and its object. It is a transmutation of the *substance* of knowledge into power to know, in other words, a *truly functional growth of the spirit itself* in the learning process.

Even a person unfamiliar with the difficult problems of philosophy and psychology can make one distinction between "knowledge of culture" and all other knowledge which bears no relation to culture, whatever might be its value. In rather popular terms, it is this: Knowledge which has become culture, so to speak, no longer rattles in the stomach in undigested form. One no longer knows how this knowledge was acquired, nor where it came from. Goethe expressed this humorously and pointedly. One of his charming poems includes a picture directed against "originals." In it he says that he no longer knows on what roasts of goose or duck, etc., he fattened his belly! "Knowledge of culture" is fully digested and assimilated knowledge which has become life and function. It is not "knowledge of experience" but "knowledge of wisdom" (Meinong),[22] in which origin and derivation can no longer be traced. One of the best popular definitions of knowledge of culture is that of William James: "A knowledge about which one neither need nor can reflect." I would like to add: It is a knowledge fully prepared for every concrete situation, ready to act, which has become "second nature" and fully adapted to the concrete task and to the demand of the hour, fitting like a natural skin, not like a ready-made suit. It is not an "application" of concepts, rules, and principles to facts, but a *possession,* an immediate perception of things *in* such a perfect manner and with such relevance that the application "seems to" put to work simultaneously an infinite number of rules and concepts and resembles a *tailor-made reaction* rather than an application. The "cultured man" finds that even as *experiences* of all kinds *happen* to him, they take on shape, form, and order, and fit into a meaningfully organized *world unity,* a "microcosm." Objects stand before his eyes and spirit "in form," in meaningful, noble, and true form, without his being conscious of having given them this order. That is why knowledge of culture is, by nature, *unpretentious,* simple, humble, never sensational, quiet, unobtrusive, self-evident. It is always aware of the limits of knowledge. Haughty pride, the feeling of superiority of the man who knows, and, even more, the conceit of the uneducated are a priori indications that culture is lacking. A wise man once said to me: "A man is cultured if one cannot tell that he has studied, if he has, and if one cannot tell that he has not studied, if he has not." True knowledge of culture is thus ever cognizant of what it does *not* know. It is always that ancient, noble *"docta ignorantia"* [learned ignorance] about which the German cardinal Nicolaus de Cusa has written such a profound book; and it is, at the same time, a truly Socratic knowledge of ignorance, a "respect for the filigree of things," as Friedrich Nietzsche called it, in which we sense and apprehend that the world is so much larger and more mysterious than our consciousness. For culture, necessarily, includes a perspective, *anterior to* experience, of realms of essence, of stages and levels of being, which we know exist but which we also know are devoid of content for us. Kant is, therefore, correct in demanding that man *know* even the "limits" of his knowledge, through a special discipline which he called "the critique of reason," and that man sharply distinguish these conscious limitations from the mere "barriers" of knowledge inherent in animals. The animal surely has no idea of what it does *not* know. It is mute and blind in knocking against the barriers imposed on it, like the goldfish hitting the walls of his glass bowl.

If we want to advance beyond these popular, pretty descriptions of knowledge of culture, if we want to grasp it *theoretically*, we might give this definition: Knowledge of culture is *knowledge of essence*, derived and organized on the basis of *one*, or a few, good and striking examples of a phenomenon, a knowledge which has become form and rule of perception and "category" of all fortuitous phenomena of similar future experience. *Each cultural group* in history, whatever its name, *possesses* (in its spirit and attitude) just such forms and patterns which it has evolved and acquired, indeed, a whole world of such forms, not only of thought and perception, but also of love and hate, taste and feeling for style, value judgment and desire. We study these forms in the history of ideas. The supreme objective of the history of ideas could well be to analyze these forms, as we find them in coherent cultural groups, in their work and achievements, and to understand the historical changes and the sequence of these patterns. Wilhelm Dilthey has recognized this in his studies in the history of ideas, for which he is justly famous. He did not, however, succeed in perceiving the *way* such patterns *develop*. Under the pressure of social and historical conditions, this same development of cultural patterns also occurs in the *individual*, in his particular cultural growth. It is, after all, always an *elite of individuals* which *first* causes the many, the masses, on their different cultural levels, to develop patterns of culture. The sociology of knowledge permits us to understand clearly in what time sequence such growth of patterns took place, how much time it took for it to penetrate beyond the elite and descend into the various levels of the masses.

This growth of patterns involves not only the mind, thought, and perception, but also our *emotional* functions, what the people call the "heart." There is such a thing as a formed culture of the heart, the will, the character, and thus we find evidence of the "heart," an *"ordre du coeur"* [order of the heart], a *"logique du coeur"* (Pascal), tact and *"esprit de finesse"* [sensitiveness] in feeling and value judgment. We find a *pattern of emotional acts* which is historically quite changeable but still of *a priori* nature as compared with fortuitous experience; its origins are essentially identical with those of patterns of the mind. Goethe acquired a certain *rhythm* of love, of felicitous enjoyment and harsh renunciation, of the "beautiful moment" which the heart hopes will last, and of the feeling that it is our holy duty to pass on to the infinite distance of self-development and spiritual action. It is probable that Goethe derived this rhythm, which, all his life, he felt to be the substance of the tragic element in life, from one *single* experience, the simple experience of Sesenheim with Friederike. Nevertheless it remained, into his old age, the form and pattern of his love for all women and also the form and pattern of his conception of *all* tragic elements in the world.

This knowledge and experience of essence is the source of the knowledge of culture which develops as its function and becomes, so to speak, its blood and life. Let us now investigate how this knowledge of essence fits into the *system of the varieties of human knowledge* which we can sketch here only in its vague outlines.

It is difficult to speak of the varieties of knowledge without establishing a general and *highest concept of knowledge*. The philosophic theory of knowledge unfortunately presents us not with one, but with many such concepts, quite different from each other. Knowledge and perception, says the school of the older dogmatists, are the reproduction of things which exist outside of our consciousness. No, says the school of Marburg, perception is the production in thought of objects according to the intrinsic rules of thought itself. The school of southwest Germany says, however: Perception is the shaping of materials through judgment. Then pragmatism states: Perceiving is judging in order to arrive at useful actions. According to Bergson, perception is the natural introduction of the feeling self into the evolution of the world. "Critical" realism believes that perception means to grasp the relationships between concepts. While concepts as such are not equivalent to objects, we must grasp them in such a manner that, at least, the relationships between objects equate the relationships between concepts. Some positivists say: Perception merely means to describe perceptible circumstances with a minimum of concepts and principles which make further direct observation unnecessary, in other words, to discover a relatively known pattern in unknown circumstances and to designate what we find with a well-defined symbol. There are as many theories as schools. It is not our present task to judge their relative merits.[23]

The mistake of *all* these attempts is that they do not start from the simple question: *What is knowledge?* For perception itself is but the conscious possession of something *"as something,"* the coincidence of a conceptual content with a meaning *independent* of it. The philosophical definitions cited above simply do not hit upon the most general concept of knowledge as the aim of all perception. Knowledge, as such, must be defined without the use of any special aspect of knowledge and without concepts which themselves include knowledge or even "consciousness" (e.g., judgment, conception, conclusion, etc.), i.e., knowledge must be defined in purely *ontological* terms.

We say: *Knowledge is an ontological relationship*, one which assumes that entity and part are forms of being. In this relationship, one being *partakes* in the circumstance of another, without causing this circumstance to change. What is "known" becomes "part" of the person who "knows," but without displacing the other person and without itself changing in any way. This ontological relationship is established without reference to space, time, and causality. Our unknown quantity is the *"mens,"* or "spirit," that sum total of acts in the "knowing" being which makes possible this partaking, which makes the existing object, or rather the *circumstance*, and *only* the circumstance, of the being who knows into an *"ens intentionale"* [being with a purpose], as distinguished from its simple *existence* (*"ens reale"*). Its existence, always and necessarily, remains *outside and beyond* the realm of knowledge.[24] The unknown quantity, spirit, is the factor which determines all movement and all acts that might bring about such *participation*. The source of this unknown quantity can only be an *active participation* which transcends itself and its own being. We call it "love" in the most formal sense. Knowledge can thus be found only where circumstantial existence occurs not only *extra mentem*, that is, *in re* outside of the spirit, in the physical shape, the thing, but also, and simultaneously, *in mente*, as *ens intentionale* and as "object" of knowledge.[25] Do we get to perceive things through our so-called "consciousness," and how do we come to perceive them? This question is not yet pertinent: "Consciousness," or knowledge of knowing (*con-scientia*) *presupposes* ecstatic knowledge (found in children, primitives, and animals). Consciousness is produced by an act of reflection, and this act, in turn, depends on the acts that constitute knowledge.

If the being that "knows" lacks an *outgoing quality,* the desire to *partake* in another being, "knowledge" is not possible at all. I can think of no other name for this desire than *"love,"* dedication, and, so to speak, a bursting of the frontiers of one's own being and circumstance through love. *The same* circumstance is grasped in the two principal categories which make up our spirit, perception and thought, i.e., grasping picture and meaning. This circumstance *"itself,"* strictly speaking, is grasped (although either wholly or in part) when meaning and object seen *completely coincide;* in other words, when the partial impressions transmitted by the various modal functions—seeing, hearing, etc.—*coincide* with each other and with memories and expectations, and when, by analogy, the several partial impressions coincide with each other so as to permit us to complete the *objective* "meaning" of the thing through successive impressions and thus form a total meaning. In this *experience of coincidence* (evidence) between perception and meaning, or, in this succession of coincidental experiences, the circumstance of the òbject "itself" becomes ever more *evident* to the spirit. Activities of thought, observation, etc., are not "themselves" knowledge, only processes *leading* to "knowledge."

If we keep to this paraphrase of "knowledge," in the most general sense of the term, the following is clear: Since knowledge is an ontological relationship, its concrete *aim,* the "purpose" of knowing and of seeking knowledge, cannot itself be knowledge, but must, in fact, be a *process of growth, of change.* It is, therefore, pointless to refuse to consider the "wherefore" ot knowledge and to say, *"la science pour la science"* [knowledge for its own sake], as is often done by those who show a completely negative attitude toward pragmatism. Epicurus said very justly that it is pure "conceit" to want knowledge only for the sake of knowledge. The autosuggestion of scholarly vanity is really no answer to a serious philosophical question! Knowledge, like everything we love and seek, must have a *value* and an ultimate *ontological meaning.* "Knowledge for the sake of knowledge" is just as vain and ridiculous as *"l'art pour l'art"* [art for art's sake] of the esthetes. The answer that knowledge exists for its own sake contains only one element (no more) of a valid "attitude"; it denies the claim of philosophical pragmatism that knowledge exists only for the sake of its utility. It is, of course, true that there exists a knowledge for the sake of practical control (not utility or the utility of control), or better, which *chooses* objects and signs of objects for the sake of this control; but it must be possible to indicate another, perhaps a more valuable, "wherefore" of knowledge.

So far, we have found only that knowledge serves *growth*. Questions arise: Growth *from what?* Growth *of what?* Growth *for what purpose?*

I believe that there are *three supreme purposes of growth* which knowledge can and should serve: First, *the growth and full development of the person* who "knows." That is *"knowledge of culture."* Second, the growth of the *world* and the timeless growth of its ultimate *source itself* of circumstance and existence, which attain their "purpose" only in our human knowledge and in all possible kinds of knowledge, or, at least, attain something in them *without* which they cannot fulfill their purpose of growth. This knowledge for the sake of God, of the *ens a se* [being by itself], we shall call *"knowledge of salvation or of grace."* Then there is a third objective of growth, practical control and transformation of the world, designed to accomplish our human aims and purposes. This is the knowledge which so-called pragmatism considers so exclusively and one-sidedly. It is the knowledge of experimental "science," the *"knowledge of control or achievement."*

Now, is there an *objective hierarchy* among these three supreme aims of growth which knowledge supports? I have in mind a very clear hierarchy which is immediately self-evident: knowledge of control which, in a practical way, serves the transformation of the world and all achievements by which we can change it and leads us to the next higher purpose, "knowledge of culture." This knowledge enables us to enlarge and unfold the being and circumstance of our spiritual person into a *microcosm* as we try, in the manner appropriate to our unique individuality, to partake in the totality of the world, or, at least, in its essential structural patterns. From "knowledge of culture" our path leads to "knowledge of salvation." That is *the* knowledge by which the nucleus of our person seeks to partake in ultimate being and the *very* source of all things; or it is the knowledge through which such participation in the ultimate source itself is accorded; or else, the knowledge in which the supreme source of all things, in so far as it "knows" itself and the world, in us and through us, *itself* attains its timeless aim of growth. First Spinoza, later Hegel and Eduard von Hartmann advanced this theory. The source of the world here achieves a kind of *union* with itself and is saved from inherent "tension" and "fundamental self-contradiction." [26] Thus, so-called "knowledge only for the sake of knowledge" exists *nowhere* and *may* and *should* not exist. Strictly speaking, it has never existed anywhere in the world.

Of these three ideals of knowledge, the recent history of the *Occident* and of its cultural annexes with independent development (America, etc.) has systematically, and ever more exclusively, cultivated only *knowledge of achievement* which wants to explore the practical possibilities of changing the world. It has encouraged the specialized experimental sciences. Knowledge of culture and knowledge of salvation have been increasingly relegated to the background in the recent history of the Occident; but even in the realm of knowledge of control and work, this period has only cared for *one of two possible* aspects, that designed to control and guide *external* (above all, inorganic) nature. The technique of controlling the *inner* life, the soul, i.e., the task of extending, as far as possible, the control and dominance of the will and, through it, of the spirit, to include the processes of the psychophysical organism in as far as it is organically constituted as a rhythmic unit of time and does not pertain to essence —this task has been vastly neglected as compared with the desire to dominate external and inanimate nature (also the inanimate nature within the organism). Only in very recent times has a strong movement in this direction originated in Europe and America. Its influence is gradually being felt in our country also. Modern Europe is far ahead of Asia in scientific knowledge designed to control external nature. The *Asiatic cultures,* on the contrary, are equally far ahead in developing knowledge of culture and of salvation and the knowledge of control involving techniques of mastering the organic, vital world. Positivism and pragmatism are no more than very one-sided *formulations* of the true state of mind in present-day Occidental knowledge and culture. Without realizing it, they make knowledge of work the only possible form of knowledge. Of these two schools, pragmatism has the very significant advantage of being *conscious* of its restricted purposes. It is far less of a hindrance in overcoming the tremendously one-sided emphasis on experimental science. The positivists, representatives of *"la science pour la science,"* in fact, devote their efforts only to knowledge of work, i.e., to a discipline which, when it does *not* serve the technological transformation of the world, is objectively meaningless and altogether without purpose, quite apart from the dubious psychological motives of its scholars. They *pretend* that their discipline is "theoretical" and purely contemplative instead of admitting its purely practical nature. Thus, illegitimately, they give it the place reserved, in the human spirit, for the development of knowledge of culture and of salvation. Against this tendency of positivism we must, therefore, always uphold the *relative* superiority of the pragmatic theory of knowledge in its interpretation of the *experimental* sciences.[27] Only when this has been done can one, so to speak, rediscover *pure* knowledge of culture and knowledge of salvation, as well as the true purposes of these two forms of knowledge, the basic spiritual attitudes which produce them, their ways of thought and perception, their methods and techniques, as if one were to pull them out from under the rubble of a civilization devoted only to work and achievement.

In order to recognize the *special nature of knowledge of culture,* we must understand, above all, that even though science and philosophy must cooperate closely, their *aims* and standards of knowledge are *antithetical.* Philosophy,[28] according to the pertinent statement of Aristotle, begins with the spiritual act of *wonderment* that this or that object of such constant nature *exists* "at all." Philosophic thinking, in the last analysis, always comes to ask: What source and cause of the world entity is needed to explain "this particular object" and also the essential structure of the world? In *"philosophia prima"* [first philosophy], the object of study is the a priori structural essence of the world. In metaphysics, the ever renewed problem is: What *did* produce this or that manifestation of such an *essence?*

Experimental knowledge of achievement and work, on the contrary, begins *its* quest, *not* with wonderment, but is impelled (by what is unaccustomed, new, and by what departs from the "regular" chain of events) to look for ways in which the reappearance of this "new" happening can be "expected," predicted, and also practically created, or, at least, *reconstituted in thought,* produced, or how one might *"manufacture"* it. "Science" is fully satisfied if the "new" and surprising elements are incorporated into the ideas concerning the regular course of events, and if the "laws of nature" are defined so as to show the event as a "consequence" of these laws, occurring under conditions which can be predicted with precision, and if the event thus proves to be relatively familiar.

This is precisely where the realm of philosophical questions *begins.* In dealing with nature, philosophy is *not* concerned with laws governing the coincidence in space and time of phenomena which can be measured mathematically and where quantities can be determined. On the contrary, it asks for the permanent *"essence"* and for what might have caused objects embodying this essence to become effective. It asks, furthermore: What is the *meaning* and *purpose* of phenomena *in general,* independent of their relationships in space and time, and of their size? Philosophy then asks concerning these relationships: *What are they?* What do they mean? *What* is their essential effect? Thus, the search for this kind of knowledge must, with the same application and precision, with the necessary assistance of its own peculiar spiritual *technique,* learn to disregard circumstance here and now and the possibility of controlling and guiding objects of all kinds as well as its own growth. By analogy, the search for the other kind of knowledge of work and achievement has to emphasize and choose in events the elements "which can be controlled," and must, conversely, purposely refrain from touching on the *essence* of things. This means: Philosophy begins when we have consciously *excluded all* possible *attitudes* reflecting *worldly desire* and *practical concerns,* those realms in which we exclusively face fortuitous existence and the reality of objects; and when we have consciously excluded the method of experimental science which chooses the objects of its knowledge in the order in which they can most easily be controlled.[29] Both when we applied *and* when we excluded the method of experimental science, our action was conscious and *willful*. *This* is what matters, if man is to care for and cultivate *all* aspects of the knowledge which he, as man, is capable of attaining.

All possible practical attitudes toward the world are conditioned by man's vitalistic aspects. Experimental science, intent on controlling the environment, excludes those human aspects which pertain only to the senses and motor mechanisms, but depends on "the" vitalistic sphere of the subject who acquires knowledge, *particularly* on his desire for control. Therefore, we can define philosophy as an attempt to attain a kind of knowledge in which facts are *no longer relative because they depend on life, not* relative to its range of values. Science must investigate objects precisely, without any reference to their essence. It must *avoid* such problems as methodically as the realm of *absolute* reality. *Its* concern is the world of "fortuitous circumstance," its "laws," *and also* the vitalistic world *"related to existence."* Problems insoluble by observation and measurement, and by mathematical logic, are *not* for experimental science; they are "meaningless" from its point of view. Conversely, a problem which can be resolved in this manner, i.e., a problem in which the solution depends on the *quantity* of inductive experience, is never an ontological problem and therefore *not* primarily one concerning philosophy. The standard of measurement, true-false, is valid for all knowledge derived from value judgment and is common to all knowledge so formulated, but philosophy has, in addition, other *decisive* standards of measurement: *first,* those on the a priori (essential) level of what is a priori true or false. *Second,* those on the level of absolute being contained in objects of knowledge. The first of these standards is supreme and decisive in awakening the *spiritual powers of the person,* i.e., *knowledge of culture;* the second, in forming knowledge of salvation, knowledge of ultimate metaphysical reality.

Let us sum up what we have said. The person who knows and discerns "much" of the fortuitous circumstance of things (*polymathia* [knowledge of many facts]) and the person with the greatest ability to predict and control development around him are, respectively, the "scholar" and the "explorer," but they are not *"cultured."* The cultured person is one who has acquired in the world *a personal structure,* an inclusive concept of ideally mobile patterns superimposed on each other, in order to arrive at *one single* way to view the world, to think, comprehend, judge, and deal with the world and *any* of its fortuitous manifestations—patterns *anterior* to fortuitous experience, capable of utilizing and integrating this experience into the entity of their personal *"world."* This is knowledge of culture. Knowledge of salvation, however, can only be devoted to the existence, essence, and value of what is absolutely real in all things. It is metaphysical knowledge.

None of these types of knowledge can ever "replace" or "be a substitute for" another. If one of them stifles *one* or *both* of the others, so as to become the only valid and effective kind of knowledge, the unity and harmony of the entire cultural existence of man is severely damaged, and so is the unity of his dual nature of body and spirit. Today, an exclusive knowledge of work and achievement supports our entire civilization, all technology, industry, and communication in space between nations and peoples. Through the recent achievements of Einstein, it even aims to define the ultimate absolute constant of nature. It aims to be valid regardless of the vantage point, in space and time, of the observer; eventually, even for inhabitants of other stars. Knowledge of achievement thus strives to attain a conception of the world that would enable man to direct the world process according to *any practical purpose* that a living and active spiritual creature might *possibly* adopt. This desire is as titanic as it is successful, and its past success has already completely transformed the conditions of man's existence. Here we are facing two false interpretations. It is wrong to deny the tremendous value of this scientific enterprise. It is equally erroneous to believe that it can take on real value only if one denies its original, practical *objective* of controlling the world in as far as possible and pretends that scientific knowledge is "pure," absolute knowledge, the only knowledge accessible to man, which it clearly is *not*. The first of these false estimates is characteristic of a false and weak-minded *romanticism;* the second, of a false and superficial *positivism* and *pragmatism*.

In the past, each great civilization has developed the three kinds of knowledge in a one-sided fashion. India has cultivated knowledge of salvation and the vitalistic, spiritual technique of achieving self-control. China and Greece championed knowledge of culture. The Occident, since the beginning of the twelfth century, has emphasized the knowledge of work of experimental, specialized science. However, the hour for *adjustment* has come and these *one-sided directions* of spiritual development must begin to *supplement* each other. The future of human culture will be marked by such adjustments and additions, not by the biased rejection of one kind of knowledge to favor another, nor by the exclusive preoccupation of each civilization with what is historically "peculiar" to it. *No* false romanticism, whether Christian, Indian, or from other regions of the "Orient," will ever again extinguish the brightly burning torch of rational world order, that powerful torch of life which first kindled Greek Pythagorean natural science, and which, while one cultural epoch of the Occident gave way to another, grew into a flame illuminating the whole world. It is still perceptible, since the "milieu" of Western man is directly or indirectly based on logical thought.

Still, it must be recognized that *these* flames will *never*, at any time in their future progress, bestow on the *nucleus of our soul,* i.e., on the *spiritual person* in man, the light and quiet glow which those flames need to feed themselves and to continue to burn. It is, indeed, possible for man to attain an ideal perfection in the methods of experimental science and to remain absolutely empty as a *spiritual being*. Man may even sink back to a kind of barbarism, compared with which all so-called primitive peoples would seem like cultured "Hellenes"! Knowledge of work, devoted to the capabilities of man as a vitalistic being, must, in the last analysis, *be subservient* to knowledge of culture. The growth and transformation of physical nature must serve the *growth* of the profound center of man, his spiritual *person*. All learning of working techniques must be subservient to the attainment of cultural knowledge and must not dominate it. A systematic and scientifically supported barbarism would indeed be the most terrifying of all imaginable barbaric conditions.

However, even the "humanistic" idea of the knowledge of *culture*, in Germany most nobly personified by Goethe, must further be subordinated to the idea of knowledge of *salvation* and must serve *it* in its ultimate purposes; for all knowledge, in the final analysis, is *from* God and *for* God.

III Spinoza

In the southern part of Amsterdam, where the river Amstel enters the city, the Jewish population had been living, since the outset of the seventeenth century, in a freely chosen ghetto called *"Judenbuurt."* After a painful exodus from Spain and Portugal, the famous Jewish clan of Maran had found a home and tolerance in the new "Jerusalem," as the Jews themselves thankfully came to call Amsterdam. The edict of 1612, prohibiting Jewish services, was repealed by Hugo de Groot on August 13, 1619. After 1657, the States General recognized the Jewish refugees in Holland as full citizens.

In the curious, colorful, and dirty ghetto of Amsterdam, Oriental in appearance, still marveled at by tourists, Baruch d'Espinoza (later baptized Benedictus) was born on November 24, 1632. His mother tongue was Castilian. He lived to be only 44. On February 21, 1677, he died at The Hague, leaving no money or possessions, except one ducat and a few silver coins.[1]

In this short span of time, Spinoza composed several works which were destined to enlighten the world. In his youth, his mind was formed and educated in the tradition of Jewish scholarship which he absorbed as a pupil in the Jewish communal school, established in 1639. His boyhood studies gave him the tools to write a Hebrew grammar, besides his metaphysical tracts, and to become the co-founder of a more scientific exegesis of the Bible which rejected all allegorical interpretations of the Scriptures and tried to proceed with strictly philological and historical methods. His school acquainted him with the Talmud and the cabala, the collective work of Jewish scholasticism and mysticism in the Middle Ages. The Arabic Aristotelianism, which was incorporated into the cabala and reached its climax in the pantheism of Averroes, prepared the way for some of

NOTE: Speech delivered at Amsterdam to commemorate the 250th anniversary of the death of the philosopher, February, 1927.

his later ideas. After Franciscus van den Enden and his beautiful daughter Clara Maria taught him Dutch and Latin, he buried himself in the writings of the great philosophers of the Occident, especially in contemporary authors, and also in mathematics and natural science. He also became familiar with later scholasticism, linked to the name of the great Spanish Jesuit, Suarez (see *Cogitata metaphysica*[2]). He did not derive his pantheism solely from the cabala. Even more significant was the influence of Neo-Platonism, the school of Florence, of Marsilio Ficino, Pico della Mirandola, of Tauler and Jacob Böhme, but especially of the great and dynamic pantheist of the Renaissance, Giordano Bruno.

However, only by combining these studies intimately with sober, rigorously mathematical, natural science, with the principles developed since Leonardo, Ubaldi, and Galileo, did he acquire the spiritual framework for his own great system. All these sources were overshadowed by the profound influence exercised by René Descartes. It could not be otherwise. The more Spinoza rose from the obscurities and chaos of the tradition of Jewish scholarship to the radiant world of Occidental thought, the more urgently he had to escape the restrictive ban of Jewish thought. When he wrote the so-called *Short Treatise*[3] in the late 1650's, the doctrines of Jewish religion already lay behind him and had congealed into materials for purely historical-critical studies. After strange disputations with the rabbis of the community, to whom Spinoza openly revealed his convictions, the grand excommunication was pronounced in the synagogue, on July 27, 1656. One passage of this document reads: "Be he damned by day and damned by night, damned when lying down to sleep and damned when arising, damned when he goes out and damned when he returns."

Uprooted from the Jewish community, he formed and educated *himself* as rarely any man has done. He sought new friends among the Dutch and the world at large. When he published his book on Cartesian philosophy, he gave the following reason for appearing in print: "On this occasion, a few men will perhaps be found in important posts in my country, who will want to see the other works I have written, the opinions I hold, and therefore will enable me to publish them without fear of annoyance." He is addressing himself here to Jan De Witt and his circle. De Witt had taken over the government when the house of Orange lost its power in 1650. The *Tractatus theologico-politicus,* a masterpiece both of political theory and philosophy of religion, has been established by Karl Gebhardt as the intellectual fruit of Spinoza's association with the circle of the retired councilman, De Witt, under whose noble protection the philosopher lived the happiest years of his life.[4]

Spinoza corresponded with almost all the great scholars of his day, and also with humbler men in his environment. Goethe called this *Correspondence,* "the most interesting book in the world of uprightness and love for man, which one can read." [5] The *Correspondence* is indeed the best source by which to judge Spinoza's human and spiritual character. Standing aloof from Judaism, and even further removed from organized Christianity of all kinds, he can say: "I take pleasure in life and spend it, not in sadness and sobbing, but in quiet, joy, and cheerfulness, and thus climb upward step by step." Spinoza's life follows this motto, a brave and wise life, striving for purest virtue and utter truth, free from desires. His sovereign self, which he knew was resting in God and protected by him, seemed to him far above the mere "powers" of the world, their dogmas, their pretentious and selfish demands. He was much too proud and too restrained to hate them. How wrong Nietzsche was to say about him: "Hatred of Jews gnawed on the God of the Jews. Hermit, have I recognized you?" Spinoza loved existence and life too much to hate his antagonists, and was satisfied to despise them a little. Albert Burgh, a young Dutch nobleman who had been his disciple but later, in Rome, joined the Catholic church, wrote him a letter full of popish garrulousness and the disrespectful arrogance of a new convert. Burgh resembled those who do not wish to struggle, themselves, for insight and truth, to taste, themselves, their evidence and clarity, but who would like to replace such clarity by "signs and miracles"

which would enable them to distinguish truth from falsehood externally. Burgh asks Spinoza how he knows that his *philosophy* is the
"best" among so many philosophies and religions. Spinoza answers
with words of simple earnest and inimitable dignity: "I do not pretend to have found the best philosophy, but I know that I perceive
the true one . . . for truth is the test of itself and of error."

    The philosophy of Baruch (or Benedictus, as he called himself
after baptism) Spinoza is justly referred to as *pantheism*. In his
most mature and basic work, *Ethica ordine geometrico demonstrata
[Ethics, Geometrically Demonstrated]*, he has exposed his most profound metaphysical ideas and also his great theory of man's road to
grace, to the light and freedom of the eternal, self-positing (*causa
sui*) God.

    Among the kinds of philosophical outlook which tradition calls
"pantheism," there is a whole series of types. Spinoza represents a
sharply delineated special form. The view that God inhabits the
world is not characteristic of a philosophical system "pantheistic" in
character; such "immanence" was also believed, e.g., by Saint Augustine. The essential idea is that God and the world are not related
like cause and effect, creator and creature, but that they are *identical
in substance*. The principal difference between "pantheistic" theories
lies in the *direction* in which the identification, God equals world, is
undertaken. If the metaphysical thinker sees the existence and essence of God fundamentally established in the spirit and afterward
attempts to show that the "world" is not an entity independent of
God, but only an aspect, an attitude, an ever new product of divine
action, we must call it an *"acosmic" pantheism* (cf. Hegel). On the
other hand, if the divinity is, so to say, lowered into a world already
conceptualized by the spirit and posited by it, and if the world is less
identified with God than God with the world, there arises the pattern
of a more or less *"atheistic"* pantheism. Almost the entire eighteenth
century made the mistake of branding Spinoza an "atheist" (a particularly sharp illustration is the *Antimachiavell* of Frederick the

Great). This was a misinterpretation. There has been no doubt about that since the Spinoza debate between Lessing and Jacobi, and since Herder and Goethe who revived the study of Spinoza's *Ethics* in the nineteenth century. Novalis hit the nail on the head when he spoke of "Spinoza, drunk with God." This strange man was so "drunk with God," that he almost overlooked the fortuitous *self*-being, *self*-right, and *self*-meaning of the *"world"* in his fervent yearning and ceaseless devotion to God in thought and love. This passion is scarcely hidden behind the frail "geometric method" of his presentation and proofs, a form imitated from the *Elements* of Euclid. Spinoza called his *Ethics* *"more geometrico demonstrata"* [demonstrated in a geometric manner]. His *"acosmic"* view appears in the fact that he maintained only one, the *res infinita,* of the three kinds of substance which his great teacher, Descartes, had advanced, *res infinita* (God), *res cogitantes* (souls), and *res extensae* (bodies). Spinoza reduced the last two to mere *attributes* of this *single* substance, God, in the form of divine "thought" and "extension." Thus, only God remained. His presence was more evident to Spinoza than the existence of his own ego and the external world of nature. This is reflected, also, in his attempt to think exclusively in terms of essential ideas and relationships, in his refusal to recognize any objective element of *chance,* any kind of "fortuitous existence," any corresponding method of *induction* in philosophy.

As an acosmic pantheism, the system of Spinoza belongs to two traditions; on the one hand, the extreme realistic *mysticism* which has developed in the Occident since Dionysius Areopagita and, on the other hand, the *Renaissance pantheism* in which Giordano Bruno's theory is the most important. These two schools, one of ecstatic contemplation and love for *God,* the other of joyful rediscovery of *nature,* of stormy and admiring dedication to its world of natural forms, meet in the spirit and heart of the great Spanish Jew. He tames them by introducing the sharply delineated concepts of the new mathematical-mechanical natural sciences (Galileo, Leonardo, Ubaldi, Huygens, Descartes) and dissolves them in the ice water of conceptualization and logic which, of course, was originally quite foreign to them. All this is contained and very closely intertwined in the *Ethics*.

Spinoza took his supreme *concept of knowledge* from ancient mysticism, "the union of the soul with the thing in itself," i.e., with God, in an *"amor intellectualis Dei"* [spiritual love of God] which is not discursive, but qualified by intuitive contemplation and delight in God. Therefore, Spinoza's *Ethics* sets out not merely to impart propositions and their proofs but, above all, to *lead the soul* of the reader, in a vivid and practical way, to this ideation of experience, to this continuous process of "transmuting" the world and life experience "into ideas." This spiritual process of attaining knowledge is directed toward blissful *perception of God* (*"frui Deo"* [delight in God]), a powerful exaltation of the soul which continuously inspires man and raises his spirit above the common level of daily living. Spinoza aims to produce this attitude, through which man *saves himself*, in the reader. Such is the purpose of the entire theory of emotions and of the theory that the emotions can be overcome by the force of reason, so magnificent and admirable in its simplicity, as stated in the fifth part of the *Ethics*. The purely *theoretical* material of the first, second, and third parts of the *Ethics*, the explanation of God, the soul, and the emotions posited by nature, are only preparation and, so to speak, establish the ontological conditions which make this attitude of the soul meaningful and possible. The reader who does not see this does not understand a word of the book, however erudite his investigation of the meaning and origin of the concepts. Only this explains why Spinoza gives the title, *Ethics*, to a book consisting three-quarters of ontological metaphysics and psychology, and not at all of ethics in the traditional sense. Ethics does not designate here a system of norms for human conduct, life, and will, but "a method of purifying the spirit and the heart so that God can be known." Spinoza intended his *Ethics* as a guide to *man's salvation*, not simply as a theory of metaphysical concepts. The basic prior condition for understanding the first two parts of this very difficult book is to recognize clearly the role that Spinoza assigns to moral conduct, in the narrow sense. It has, as such, no intrinsic value. It is not an ultimate aim for man. It only disposes man to conceive a purely *theoretical and contemplative objective,* the knowledge of God.

On this issue, Spinoza is about as far removed as Plato from Kant and Johann Gottlieb Fichte. For these philosophers of "freedom," the *practical* being and life of man, the free accomplishment of duty and *action* contain the ultimate *meaning* of life, and even knowledge and the theory of knowledge are subservient to this ultimate meaning. "Virtue," on the contrary, is significant for Spinoza only as a means to ultimate knowledge, *knowledge of God.* Organized religion, the "metaphysics of the masses," as Spinoza, the accomplished aristocrat and individualist, disdainfully called it, has only practical-moralistic and sociological meaning. (We find this idea thoroughly developed in the *Tractatus theologico-politicus.*) Kant, in his theory of postulates, wants to exalt religion by making it the prior condition for man's ability to fulfill the absolute demands of duty. Thus, he transforms "physical theology" into "ethical theology." Spinoza does exactly the opposite and *depreciates* religion by attaching to it only the purpose of producing moral conduct. He values his own *gnostic metaphysics,* "the religion of thinkers," far above religion.

Spinoza's acosmic pantheism means the same thing in Holland as the theories of Giordano Bruno in Italy. Nevertheless, they are *separated* by a deep gulf, because Spinoza writes entirely from the background of *mathematical-mechanical* natural sciences, in fact, in an extreme form, expressed in mathematical-geometric terms. Neither the concepts, "time" and "power," nor the concepts, "direction" and "evolution," find a place in Spinoza's "world." This is the greatest weakness of his theory. His world is entirely conceived in the way of the Eleatics. It consists of powerless, timeless, undynamic "eternal *being.*" The objects contained in the world are the eternally necessary "consequences" of God. They follow from a pattern of timeless and non-dynamic, mathematical and logical sequences of cause and effect, just as the sum of the angles results from the nature of the triangle. Reality is a timeless, eternal, and intimate relationship of causes and effects which can be fully understood and which are transparent as crystal. All forms, shapes, particulars, qualities, purposes, values, and also time do not pertain to *being* by itself. They are associated with objects only by man. In this respect, Spinoza's pantheism is quite unlike the dynamic evolutionary pantheism of the Italian Renaissance and no less different from Goethe's pantheism.

Spinoza's theory differs from the *mystical* tradition in his idea *"Deus sive natura"* [God, or its equivalent, nature], the intimate (substantial) association of God and *nature*. This becomes clearly evident when he says that, besides "thought," unlimited "extension" is one of the many attributes of God. The twelfth and thirteenth propositions of part one of the *Ethics,* and its annexes, try to show that the divisibility of God does not follow from his unlimited extension which can *neither* be measured *nor* divided. Only a definite, quantitative *condition* of bodily substance can be divided, never substance itself. Only the extensionless *essence* of extension (*extensio*) is an attribute of God, not a particular extendedness (*extensum*) which is always qualitatively realized (proposition 15).

This theory of Spinoza can be fully understood only through Descartes. Descartes had denied that extension is only an attribute of body substance; it is rather its very *essence*. A body *is* only a *piece* of extension. Therefore, physics is to be derived from a "geometry of nature." There is no empty space anterior to bodies, like an empty shell ready to receive them, and matter is not anatomical but strictly continuous. All specific patterns of space arise when motion is introduced. This theory of Descartes was not far removed from the ideas of Spinoza who believed that bodies are only forms (*modi*) of indivisible extension. "Souls" are considered in an analogous way. Descartes, though still clinging to the substantiality of finite "spirits," denied that thought was only an activity of the soul. He conceived of thought and consciousness as its *essence*. Here again we are not far from Spinoza. According to him, the soul is only a special form, the *"modus"* of *one single* and infinite divine thought. God himself thinks in us: "And a divinity spoke when I thought I was speaking, and when I believed a divinity to be speaking, I myself was speaking." *

It can easily be seen that these consequences of Cartesian philosophy make it unnecessary to "locate the soul" in the brain and to assume an "interplay" between body and soul. These assumptions must be replaced by a *parallelism of analogous concepts* which Spinoza expresses in this manner: "The order and connection of conceptions is the same as the order and connection of objects" (proposition 7, pt. II). This parallelism has, however, little in common with the modern so-called "psychophysical" parallelism of Fechner, Wilhelm Wundt, and others. For Spinoza does not think of a parallel between consciousness and mental activity; instead, he is thinking of an essential connection between conception and objects conceived. He assumes an identical order for their sequence and their other relationships.[6] Plato considered the body a "prison of the soul." Spinoza has a similar view of the body and its "emotional impulses." They are, accordingly, neither specific causes nor parallels of thoughts in man. They are only *limiting* moments which *deceive* us and lead *to error*. Expressed more simply, they are not what specifically determines rational activity, but what determines the *counterforces opposing reason*—the *emotions*. Knowledge and a life ruled by the power of reason demand, therefore, that the "confused" ideas and images, to which the emotional impulses of the body correspond, be dissolved by positive thought in man and be transformed into clear, precise, and adequate ideas. Like the gnostics, Spinoza sees error and evil as the result not of free acts of the spirit, but of a limitation of the spirit through the body.

Thus, the theories of knowledge (*Ethics*, pt. II) and of emotions (pt. III) are closely related. Man's *freedom* from emotions and his gradual liberation from emotions, through their progressive realization (a technique which Goethe deeply appreciated and applied in

---

* Goethe, *Prometheus. Dramatisches Fragment*, V, 110 f.

Werther), is only a negative guidance and determination of life through reason and, therefore, only a negative approach to true knowledge. Freedom no longer means a freedom of choice, which Spinoza's strong determinism rigorously denies. There remains no freedom to say yes or no to our conceptions and to their combinations, as Descartes had assumed. As opposed to external and internal compulsion ("emotions!"), Spinoza's freedom is only a determination of deed and action through the active and acting being itself. There is no freedom to do good or evil, but "a being *is* good and perfect to the extent that it is free," and this always means, for Spinoza, as long as it is independent and potent, not passive and impotent. Spinoza was the first to defend with utmost vigor the specifically modern idea of an autonomous ethics for "free" man which rejects all established authorities and completely excludes the motives of punishment and reward from the realm of ethics. *"Blessedness is not the reward of virtue, but virtue itself. One does not enjoy virtue because one restrains appetites, but one can restrain appetites because one possesses virtue"* (proposition 42, pt. V). In this statement, Spinoza has cast one of the most penetrating glances into the human heart.

The third part of the *Ethics* attempts to derive the entire host of emotions and passions from the simple condition of pleasure and displeasure. Spinoza would observe passions dispassionately, "as if" they constituted a geometric pattern. His analysis is often insufficient, and Nietzsche has justly ridiculed Spinoza's definition of love. Still, even in this respect, he uncovers a wealth of fundamental links between the movements of the soul, and his definitions are often admirably sharp and subtle. Incidentally, this part makes Spinoza one of the fathers of so-called associative psychology, i.e., of that school of psychology which conceives of all spiritual processes in the patterns of mechanical causality. He does not, of course, ask us to include rational activity within an associative context, as the English philosophers did later. Spinoza avoided such nonsense.

The profound part four, entitled "Of Human *Bondage*," is only a transition to part five, "Of the Power of the Intellect or Of Human Liberty." Based on the natural principles of emotions, which have been previously established, part four shows in what varied ways different emotions hinder the attainment of the aim of life, knowledge of God. In this part, the positive, joyful, truly unresentful, amoral spirit of Spinoza finds wonderful and concrete expression. His great maxim, that we should *never* try to reduce vice by fighting it negatively, by prohibition, reproof, or indignation, should be an axiom for pedagogy. For, as Spinoza says, this does more to render vice ingrained than to reduce it. Only the indirect *awakening of a new love and power for virtue* and for all positive values can be effective (see, e.g., proposition 63e, pt. IV). In this part and in the final one, the spiritual visage of Spinoza shines, ever more clear and alive, from beneath the dry formulation of the work. What light is cast on his life, e.g., by proposition 70 in part four, on his proud concern to maintain his independence! In 1663, this concern prevented him from accepting the offer of a professorship at Heidelberg, made by the elector of the Palatinate. He continued to earn his meagre living from grinding lenses. The proposition reads: "The free man living among the ignorant tries to avoid their benevolence in as far as possible."

The problem of *suffering, evil,* and wrong, discussed in part four seems strangely to fade away in the face of his powerful, joyful affirmation of life. Here Spinoza is completely a man of the Renaissance. For him, the very *fullness* of being is good. This justifies his God if one asks: "Whence and why do we have suffering, wrong, and sin?" Spinoza answers: If the divinity had forgotten suffering, wrong, and sin, it would not have let *"everything* possible" flow from itself! His insight is very profound when he observes that emotions cannot be conquered by thought alone, but only by other emotions. That is why the desire to know must become *passion, "amor intellectualis"* [spiritual love] if it is to overcome the emotions and lead man to freedom. The sociological propositions of this fourth part also contain profound and true insights. Only spiritual possessions *unify* men; sensual attributes divide them. No one has ever fully exhausted the depth of the proposition that hatred is always evil (even hatred of evil) and that "the minds of men are not won by arms, but through love and noble feelings."

In part five, Spinoza rises to the full height of his spiritual stature. The reader who follows him in this part seems automatically to *transcend* all the depravities of human existence and breathes deep draughts of the eternal air of God himself. In his peculiar and original way, Spinoza resumes the powerful tune which Plato first intoned and which resounds through all great European philosophy. It is the tune of Eros which leads the soul to God. Everything converges on the concept of *"amor intellectualis Dei."* This love is the source of Spinoza's personal nature and of his indivisible intuition of the world in its most concentrated form.

The fifth part begins with the famous indications of how man can *free* himself from emotions and thus rid himself of the obstacles to the *one* divine way of thinking. Several techniques are suggested: Distinguish the emotion sharply from the conception of the external object which arouses it! Reduce "confused conception" (the essence of emotion, according to Spinoza) into clear and precise conception! *Look at emotion objectively!* Above all, reduce it by recognizing everything which occurs in an *external determinism* as a part of the total world context, for only the isolated object arouses emotion! Where we succeed with this technique of reducing emotions by getting to know them, we see all things *"sub specie quadam aeterni"* [as some kind of aspect of the eternal], i.e., through the love of God (proposition 15, pt. V). Peace, calm, quiet, and bliss spring up in us if we derive all being, every event, from God and consider each a link of *his* eternal and necessary order. The human spirit takes such different forms that realization of this eternal determinism almost crushes a man like Johann Gottlieb Fichte who, in his youth, was, for some time, a follower of Spinoza, while it frees and calms the "Spinoza type" man and fills him with bliss. This illustrates the profound contrast between contemplative man and moral man intent

on action, on improving and changing the world. These two types
have perhaps found their purest, but also most extreme, manifestations in Spinoza and Fichte.

Spinoza's work ends with a glowing hymn to divine love. A
strangely mystical idea is daringly set forth: "The spiritual love [of
man] for God is divine love in which God loves himself," or, "spiritual love for God is a part of that infinite love in which God loves
himself." Like Goethe's Philine, in the well-known line inspired by
Spinoza, man seems to say: "If I love you, what is it to you?" Convinced that only the imperfect can love what is perfect, and the
perfect one (God) only himself, Spinoza remains true to the old
Platonic axiom of love; but in a profound adaptation of medieval
mysticism, which also spoke of *"amare Deum in Deo"* [to love God
in God], Spinoza associates this Platonic concept with the idea, ex-
traneous to antiquity, that our human love for God is only a part, a
function, of the infinite spiritual love through which God blissfully
reaffirms his being and essence throughout eternity. Subsequently,
this idea became an important influence on the later Fichte, on
Schelling, Hegel, and Eduard von Hartmann, all of whom combined
Kant's critique and subjectivism with Spinoza's philosophy by transforming Kant's Eleatic rigidity and theory of inactivity into a meaningful system in which the forms of the *divinity* evolve throughout
history. For instance, when Hegel defines metaphysics as the *growing*
self-awareness of God *in* man, he is simply applying a fundamental
thought of Spinoza to history.

The influence of Spinoza's world of ideas on the intellectual
history of almost all European countries has been so great that it is
difficult to assess. However, it was strongest in the *German* history
of ideas. It started in Germany at the moment when the German
spirit and its outstanding *elites*, in classical and romantic literature
and in the lofty philosophy emanating from Kant, in Johann Gottlieb Fichte, Schelling, Hegel, and Eduard von Hartmann, began to
overcome *at the same time* the utilitarian ideas of rationalistic en-

lightenment and the threadbare dogmatism of the established church and Christianity, and when the German spirit was beginning to create for itself a new world out of the depths of its national soul. When Fritz Jacobi, in the essay on Spinoza's philosophy, called him an atheist, Goethe commented that, for him, Spinoza was "the firmest believer in God, *theissimus.*" After the very first reading of the *Ethics,* Goethe said: "A great and free view of the world of senses and ethics has been opened to me. I have never had the impression of perceiving the world so clearly." He called Spinoza his "lord and master," and even in his old age he considered Spinoza, Linnaeus, and Shakespeare the authors who "exercised the greatest influence" on him. Like Spinoza, Goethe justly banned all "utilitarian explanations" from natural science; also like Spinoza, he rejected ideas of the fall, of original sin, and of accompanying salvation, because they seemed adverse to his nature. Spinoza accompanied him throughout life. He spiritualized and permeated Goethe's art as well as his nature studies. Before Goethe, Lessing had died as a "Spinozist." Lessing shared the views Spinoza set forth, in his *Tractatus theologico-politicus,* concerning revelation and established religion: they have value for the masses and for popular education, but not in the search for truth. The greatest Protestant theologian of the nineteenth century, Friedrich Schleiermacher, emphatically exclaimed in his *Discourses on Religion:* "Make the pious offering of a lock of the manes of the holy exile, Spinoza." The reference to the *"holy* Spinoza" became a favorite in those great days of the German spirit.

In spite of the glorification of Spinoza, which is as predominant in our era as were disdain and lack of comprehension in the eighteenth century, the advance of technical philosophy has noted many profound and incurable weaknesses in his work. But, whatever Spinoza's thought will mean for the future of philosophy and especially of metaphysics, *two* things are *aere perennius* [perennial] in his work: First, the eminent *spiritual stature* of this great *man,* so very solitary and pure, which greets us in the chiseled sentences of the

Ethics. His spirit will be a radiant example for kindred minds and friends; and it is only for "friends" that one can philosophize. Second, the value of *cleansing and purification*. For willing minds, it means that Spinoza forcefully guides men's souls to the realm of freedom, light, and proximity to God.

IV Man and History

If there is a philosophical task for which our era demands a solution with unique urgency, it is that of philosophical anthropology. I am referring to a basic science which investigates the *essence* and *essential constitution* of man, his relationship to the realms of nature (organic, plant, and animal life) as well as to the source of all things, man's metaphysical origin as well as his physical, psychic, and spiritual origins in the world, the forces and powers which move man and which he moves, the fundamental trends and laws of his biological, psychic, cultural, and social evolution, along with their essential capabilities and realities. Herein resides the psychophysical problem of body and soul, and the noetic-vitalistic problem. Only such an anthropology can furnish an ultimate philosophical basis, as well as definite, certain aims of research, to all sciences concerned with the object, "man," to the natural, medical, archeological, ethnological, historical, and social sciences, to normal and developmental psychology and character analysis.

The views concerning *the essence and origin of man* have, at no other time, been less sure, less determinate, and more varied, than in our own. Long and thorough investigations of the problem of man should give the author the right to assert this. In approximately ten centuries of history, this is the first in which man finds himself completely and utterly "problematical," in which he no longer knows what he is and simultaneously *knows that* he does not have the answer. We can attain valid insights again only if we are willing, for once, to clear away all traditional solutions and to look at the being, called man, with an extreme and methodical objectivity, and wonder. But everyone knows how difficult such a *tabula rasa* [clearing of the mind] will be, since hardly any other problem finds us holding more

NOTE: First published in the monthly, *Die neue Rundschau* (November, 1926).

unconsciously, and therefore more violently, to traditional categories. In order to slowly shake off these categories, all we can do is investigate their precise cultural origins and overcome them by realizing their presence.

In doing so, a *history of man's consciousness of self,* a history of the ideal, basic forms in which man thought, saw, and felt himself, and through which he placed himself into the patterns of being, should precede the study of ideas about man in myth, religion, theology, and philosophy. Without entering into such a history, which is to be the introduction to the author's *Anthropologie,* let us point out one thing. The fundamental direction of this history is clear— the *growth* of human consciousness of self. It moves ahead in ever renewed bounds at critical points in history. Backward motions, found here and there, are not very significant to the basic trend. Primitive peoples are not the only ones who still feel quite related and close to the world of animals and plants that surrounds their society and living area. A high civilization, like that of India, is also based on an unquestionable feeling of unity between man and life of *all* kinds. India, as well, places plant, animal, and man, as cumulative units, equals, and relatives, beside one another into *a great democracy of being.* The sharp distinction between man and nature, in experience and feeling, in thought and theory, did not arise before the height of classical Greek civilization.[1] For here, and *only* here, the idea of *Logos, reason,* and *spirit* was coined. This spirit is regarded as the unique, specific attribute of man. It is said to raise him high above and beyond all living creatures and to relate him to the divinity itself, in a way of which no other being is capable. Christian doctrine, which refers to the divine nature of man and considers men as children of God, generally represents another rise in the consciousness of the human self. Whether Christian man thinks well or ill of himself, in either case, he attributes to himself, as man, a cosmic and metacosmic significance which the Greek or Roman of classical antiquity would never have dared assume.

The beginning of modern thought meant a new jump upward

in the history of man's consciousness of self even though, increasingly, he saw through medieval anthropomorphism. It is a widespread error, for instance, to assume that the thesis of Copernicus, when it first appeared, was considered a reason to diminish and decrease human consciousness of self. Giordano Bruno, the greatest missionary and philosopher of the new astronomical cosmology, gave voice to the opposite feeling. Copernicus merely discovered a new star in the heavens, the earth. Bruno thought himself authorized to shout out ecstatically: "We *are* therefore already in heaven," and do not need the heaven of the church. God is not the world, but, rather, the *world itself is God*. This was the new thesis of the acosmic pantheism of men like Bruno and Spinoza.[2] The Middle Ages saw the world existing independently of God and believed in the creation of the world and the soul. These conceptions were false, according to Bruno and Spinoza. *This* identification of the world with God, and not a lowering of God toward the world, was characteristic of the new mentality. It is true that Renaissance man realized that he was merely the inhabitant of a small planet circling the sun. However, the fact that his reason had the power to penetrate the natural appearances of the senses and to investigate their hidden aspects significantly increased man's consciousness of self.

With Descartes and modern philosophy, reason, characteristic of man since the Greeks, enters into a new basic relationship with God. Duns Scotus and Suarez had, so to speak, elevated man's metaphysical rank by ascribing to his spiritual soul the predicates that Thomas Aquinas had specifically granted only to the *"angelus,"* to *"forma separata,"* and to *"substantia completa"* [angels, separate forms, complete substance], namely, the individuation of man without an individuating *"prima materia"* [divine substance], individuation through man's spiritual being itself. But since Descartes and the tremendous declaration of independence of thought in his *"cogito ergo sum"* [I think, therefore I am], human consciousness of self has passed the bounds set by medieval thinkers. The great mystics of the thirteenth and fourteenth centuries had come close to equating

consciousness of self and consciousness of God. These concepts penetrate each other so thoroughly in Descartes that there is no further
need to derive the existence of God from that of the world, as did
Thomas Aquinas. On the contrary, the world itself is derived from
the primordial light of reason which knows that it is directly anchored
in the divinity. The pantheists, from Averroes to Spinoza, Hegel, and
Eduard von Hartmann, assumed the partial identity of human and
divine spirit as one of their fundamental doctrines. For Leibnitz also
man is a small God.

One of the fundamental tasks of philosophical anthropology is
to investigate what the periodic advances in human consciousness of
self signify. There are two antithetical questions. Do these advances
mean that man grasps his real place in the world, and his situation
with respect to the totality of being, with an ever deeper and truer
insight? Or do they mark the progress and growth of a dangerous
illusion; are they the symptoms of an increasing disease?

Two problems will not concern us here. First, the history of
human consciousness of self or its critical analysis. Second and particularly, all questions of fact and truth in anthropology. All we
shall give here is a small segment of an introduction to a compre-
hensive anthropology. Our aim is to explain only the *present* intellectual context of the problem. We shall describe a few, to be exact,
five, basic types of man's conception of himself, in order to outline, as
sharply as possible, the various interpretations of the nature of man,
as found today in our Western civilization. We shall further show
how a particular kind of *historical approach,* i.e., a basic concept of
human history, specifically characterizes each of these ideas. The
reader is asked emphatically not to assume that the author stands
"closer" to one, or the other, of the five conceptions, or even that he
might consider one of them true. What the author himself holds to
be true and correct will be explained in the principal part of his
Anthropologie, and not in his short essay which intends only to
orient the reader and relate ideas.[3]

First, however, a word concerning the *relationship* between *anthropology and history.*

The most important reason that so many and such different conceptions of history and sociology are in bitter struggle with each other today is that these conceptions of history are based on fundamentally different ideas of the nature, structure, and origin of man. For, whether or not the historian, sociologist, or philosopher of history is conscious and aware of it, each historical doctrine is based on a particular kind of anthropology. We no longer have any agreement in our views of man's nature. Let us be satisfied to study what ideas concerning man and his place in the fullness of being, are alive today in our Occidental civilization. Let us reduce them to the sharpest and most understandable basic types. We shall find, as thorough research has led me to see, *five fundamental ideas.* Within their framework, of course, individual anthropological theories can still be unusually varied, in view of the many different problems with which "anthropology" must deal. Three of the five ideas are quite familiar in circles of general culture, even though we rarely find them in sharply delineated form. Two of them, the newest and most recent, are still unknown to those trained in the field because they are so unusual and different. Each of these ideas is accompanied by a special conception of history. Let us sketch the five ideas in the following sections.

I

The first conception of man is still widely prevalent in all theistic circles (Jewish or Christian), especially in those affiliated with the church. It is not a product of philosophy or science, but an idea of *religious faith.* It represents a very complex result of religious Judaism and its testimonials, especially the Old Testament, the religious histories of antiquity, and the Gospels. Its well-known mythos includes the creation of man (in body and soul) by a personal

God, man's descent from a first couple, his stay in paradise (doctrine of origins), original sin committed when man was seduced by an angel who fell of his own free will, salvation through the God-man with his dual nature who thus re-established the condition of men as children of God, the colorful eschatology which speaks of freedom, personality, and spirituality, the immortality of the so-called "soul," the resurrection of the body, universal judgment, etc. Within this Judeo-Christian frame of reference, we can, of course, find theological anthropologies with fundamentally different philosophies of history, e.g., with different interpretations of the "fall of man"; for the anthropology of Judeo-Christian faith has produced an impressive variety of conceptions of history and perspectives of the world, from Augustine's *City of God* to Otto von Freising, Bossuet, and the most recent trends in theology.

It is scarcely necessary to state that, on the one hand, this religious anthropology is entirely meaningless for autonomous philosophy and anthropology and that, on the other hand, it disturbs anyone sensitive in feeling and thought to see the ancient mythos, so magnificent and meaningful, apparently supported and apologetically defended by rational argument. Let us emphasize one aspect. This mythos is far more powerful and effective among men than one might suspect. A person who no longer believes these things dogmatically is, for all that, still far from abandoning the forms and values of human consciousness of self, or the human realization of self, which have their roots in this objective presence of faith. For, feelings and forms of life which, through many centuries, produce enduring beliefs and dominant ideas far outlast these ideas themselves. Even today, the entire Occidental world, including its unbelievers, feels, for instance, the burden of fear, the nightmare, which psychologically once gave birth to the mythos of fall and original sin, the experience of infirmity, a kind of incurable disease of man as man. We find it wonderfully portrayed in the dream play of Strindberg. Kant renders it with the words: "Man is made from wood too twisted to fashion anything straight." And there has not yet appeared the great "psychoanalyst of history" who could free historical man from the fear of the world, and cure him, not of the fall of man and original sin which are mythos, but of that inherent pressure of fright, the emotion- and drive-conditioned root, which characterizes the Judeo-Christian world of ideas.

II

A second idea about man, still effective in our world, was *discovered by the Greeks,* in the Greek city states—one of the most powerful and influential discoveries of the history of human self-judgment, initiated by the Greeks and *only* by them and by no other human culture. We say this with intentional emphasis. It is, briefly, the idea of *"homo sapiens"* [rational man]. Anaxagoras, Plato, and Aristotle first expressed it as a sharp, definite, and clear philosophic concept. This idea makes a fundamental distinction between man and animal. It does not attempt, as is so often erroneously believed, merely to delimit man empirically from the animals closest to him, such as anthropoid apes, and to establish distinctive morphological, physiological, and psychological qualities. Such a procedure could never *generically* oppose man to animal and to all infrahuman nature, but only to the single chosen object of comparison, e.g., chimpanzees, orang-utangs, catarrhine primates, etc. Since there is, at least, no question that man is, e.g., infinitely closer to the chimpanzee than either of the two are to the toad or the serpent, *this* method would never provide the slightest basis for the "generic" distinction between the idea, man, and the idea, animal, conceived with reference to man. The idea, man, dominant in history, which we use ten times daily, whether we believe in it or not, is formed according to very different principles. As I have shown elsewhere in detail,[4] it follows logically when one assumes the idea of God and the doctrine that man was formed in the image of God.

Classical Greek philosophy, we might say, conceptualized this idea for the first time. Within the framework of a world view which basically interprets all being organologically, using categories of positive, efficacious, ideational form, and negative (μὴ ὄν), passive substance (*materia*), human consciousness of self, for the first time, rises above all remaining nature. Since the nature of man is assumed to be stable and, like all species, eternal, it has a *specific agent,* which pertains only to it, reason (λόγος, *ratio*), a factor which cannot be reduced to the elementary agents pertaining to plant and animal souls. Only by means of this reason will *homo* be capable of recognizing being in itself, as it is, the divinity, the world, and himself, of forming nature meaningfully by his ποιεῖν [activity], of treating his fellow-man well in his πραττεῖν [way of acting], i.e., of living so as to develop, as perfectly as possible, this specific agent of νοῦς ποιητικός [creative reason]. Early Greece, unlike almost all other cultures of the period, conceived the idea of man as comprising all races, tribes, peoples, and also classes. From Plato to the Stoics, man always used the same argument to approach being itself with his ideas. So-called reason in man is considered a *partial* function (which only later becomes a creation) of the *divine,* ideating λόγος, νοῦς, always producing anew this world and its order, not in the sense of creation, but as eternal movement and formation.

Let us attach special significance to four particular qualifications. (1) Man possesses in himself a divine agent which *none* of nature, as such, contains. (2) Nevertheless, this agent and the force which eternally shapes and forms the world into a world (rationalizes chaos, "matter," into a cosmos) are identical ontologically and in principle and, therefore, are truly adequate for knowledge of the world. (3) As λόγος (the realm of *"formae substantiales"* in Aristotle) and as human reason, this agent is potent and able to realize its ideal content ("power of the spirit," "independent power of the idea") even without the drives and senses (perception, μνήμη, etc.) common to man and animal. (4) This agent is absolutely constant, regardless of the position of the individual in history, nation, and society.

It is a fact to be especially emphasized that almost all specifically philosophical anthropology, from Aristotle to Kant and Hegel, though its development has been tremendous, has not significantly changed with respect to these four qualifications of the theory of man. In these points, Aristotle, Thomas Aquinas, Descartes, Spinoza, Leibnitz, Kant, Malebranche, etc., are in agreement, in spite of all their differences. The four principles are not affected by the opposition between theism and pantheism. In stoicism first, then in Platonic-Augustinian thought in the early Middle Ages, then in Aristotelian-Thomistic form in the later Middle Ages they assumed special historical force, because they were combined with the idea of man inspired by religious faith, which we described earlier as a preliminary basis of theology (*preambula fidei*). The manner in which they combined is immaterial. When the world of dogma became foreign to large segments of western culture, the doctrine of "*homo sapiens*" remained as the sole ruling one and saw its greatest triumphs in the century of Enlightenment.

Of the four above mentioned elements, only one, the qualification of stability, was abandoned, in opposition to the philosophy of the Enlightenment, by the greatest philosophic personality after Kant, by the thinker who most influenced conceptions of history. It was Hegel who stated, in the Introduction to his *Philosophy of History:* "The only thought, with which philosophy approaches world history, is the simple idea of reason, namely, that reason rules the world and that history has unfolded rationally." Here we find three of the qualifications given above, including an extreme, impersonal *Panlogos* and the theory that divine and human reason are fully identical, intensified to become a theory of the unlimited power of reason. There is, however, one relatively new idea. Only in the *process of becoming* does man attain, and is man *supposed* to attain, an increasing consciousness of what he has ideally been throughout eternity, the consciousness of his *freedom*, superior to his drives and his nature. Hegel denies the stability of human reason—a tremendous step ahead. He sees a history of the subjective, categorical forms and shapes of the human spirit *itself*, not just a history of cumulative achievements of reason. This history of the human spirit itself is independent, in Hegel, from the biological changes of human nature. This history is the evolution of the eternal divinity which becomes conscious of itself and of its eternal, categorical, and ideal world in man. It is the development of the Greek λόγος made historically dynamic. Drives and passions are introduced only as servants of the Logos, as "malice of the idea," i.e., as cleverly chosen tools of the divine idea, through which it achieves its aims, establishes a harmony and balance which no one knows, except the divinity itself and he, the philosopher, drunk with God, who meditates the divine dialectic process of history. There is neither ultimate *personal* freedom nor active leadership. The leader is nothing more than the spokesman and business executive of the world spirit. Hegel's theory of history presents us the last, highest, and most developed view of history within the framework of the anthropology of *"homo sapiens."*

One further comment. It is most important to realize that this theory of *"homo sapiens"* has become, in all of Europe, what is most dangerous for an idea, namely, self-evident. And yet, reason is for us, pending new examinations of the facts, essentially but an "invention of the Greeks." I really know only two authors who fully recognized this fact, Wilhelm Dilthey and Friedrich Nietzsche. Nietzsche saw, with outstanding insight, that the traditional idea of truth, which is the coincidence between thought and object, logically stands and falls with the spiritualistic idea of God. This idea of truth is itself but a form of the "ascetic ideal" which he aimed to overcome through his "Dionysian pessimism" and through the theory of knowledge which he defined in *Will to Power*. According to it, all forms of thought are only the tools of the human will to power. He differs sharply from scholars who, though willing to accept the dictum that "God is dead," in their life and work, pay tribute to a set of values, values of pure knowledge of truth, which make sense only if one assumes the proposition which they deny. Nietzsche radically questioned the meaning and value of what we call "truth itself." Wilhelm Dilthey does likewise when he writes: "The rationalist position is represented today principally by the school of Kant. The father of this position was Descartes, who first gave victorious expression to the sovereignty of the intellect. This sovereignty is rooted in the whole religious and metaphysical attitude of his epoch, equally present in Locke and Newton, Galileo and Descartes. It takes reason to be the principle of world order, not an episodic fact on earth. Yet today no one can escape the fact that this magnificent, religious, metaphysical background is no longer self-evident. Many forces have brought this about. Analysis of nature gradually seems less dependent on the principle of constructive reason. Laplace and Darwin most clearly represent this development. Analysis of the nature of man, likewise, seems to enable our scientific "common sense" to get along without any link between this nature and a higher order. In these two changes of view, a third is implied. The religious relationship between creator and creature is no longer a compelling fact for us. From all this, we conclude that one can no longer reject a priori an opinion which considers the sovereign intellect of Descartes a passing and unique product of nature on our earth and perhaps on other constellations. Many of our philosophers fight this view, but none considers reason the self-evident background of the entire world order. Thus, the power of this reason to take possession of reality through thought becomes a hypothesis or a "postulate." [5]

We shall now encounter two other ideas of man which are excluded by the idea of *"homo sapiens"* which we have discussed. First, *"Dionysian man"* who, like *"homo sapiens,"* consciously tries to exclude his drives and senses, in order to grasp "eternal ideas," but who, unlike him, desires nothing *more* than to eliminate the influence of the spirit, of reason (by trance, dances, and narcotics), in order to become one with creative nature, *natura naturans,* in a feeling and life of oneness. This anthropological idea considers reason to be *the* infirmity of life, and the force which separates man from the creative powers of nature and history. The second idea, no less distinct from "homo sapiens," is the *"homo faber"* [man who acts] of positivism, which denies any new and essentially spiritual force in man. We shall now briefly describe this latter theory of man.

III

Criticism has rendered this third dominant ideology of man at least as untenable as the previous ones. It is the *naturalistic,* *"positivistic,"* and later also *"pragmatic"* theory which I would like to designate by the short formula, *"homo faber."* [6] This idea also deals with all basic problems of anthropology. It is fundamentally distinct from the above mentioned theory of man as *"homo sapiens."*

This theory of *"homo faber,"* first of all, denies any separate, spiritual power of reason in man. Man and animal are not essentially different. There are only differences *of degree*. Man is a special kind of animal. In men, the same elements, forces, and laws are active as in all other beings, only with more complex consequences. This is true physically, psychologically, and in the so-called "noetic" way. Everything relating to the soul or the spirit must be understood through drives and sense perception and their genetic derivatives. The so-called thinking "spirit" is but a late epiphenomenon, an inactive reflection of forces in our consciousness, forces equally active in the subhuman animal world, and what is true for spirit applies also to the following capacities which are only apparently distinct from drives: coordinated will and set purpose, conception and appraisal of values, spiritual love, as well as the accomplishments of these forces (culture). Therefore, man is not primarily a rational being, not a *"homo sapiens,"* but a *"creature of drives."* What he calls his thoughts, his will, his higher emotional acts (love, in the sense of pure goodness), is but a kind of "symbolic conversation of his impulses" (Nietzsche, Hobbes), a symbolism of fundamental patterns of drives and of related perceptions. Man is only a highly evolved creature. What we call spirit and reason does not have an independent and separate metaphysical origin, and is not something that possesses an original and autonomous order which might directly correspond to the laws of being. It is purely a further development of the highest psychic qualities which we find in anthropoid apes. It is a further evolution of the technical *intelligence,* e.g., of the chimpanzee. It is an intelligence superior to all merely associative order and no less superior to immobile, inherited instinct. It is, in other words, the ability to adapt actively to new, atypical situations by anticipating the structure of objects in the environment without having to resort to trial and error, an ability which makes it possible to satisfy ever more directly the fundamental drives of the species and of the individual. These drives are found also among animals.[7] As in the case of all other psychological phenomena and relationships, this "technical intelligence" is accorded very specific corollaries among the functions of the nervous system, for here the spirit is only one part of the "psyche," the inner aspect of the life process. What we call knowledge is merely a series of pictures which intervene between the impulse and the reaction of the organism, in over more varied form, or an increasing number of self-made symbols for things, or of conventional relationships between these symbols. These images and series of symbols and their combinations increasingly adhere to the individual and (by heredity) to the species. They lead to successful and profitable reactions to our neighbors, which enable us to attain through our efforts what originally was the objective of our drives. We call these symbols and their combinations "true" when they bring about the success of profitable reactions. We call them "false" when they fail to do so. By analogy, actions become "good" or "bad." The unity of the Logos, which itself forms the world and simultaneously is active in us as our *ratio,* is not required, as long as one does not understand human insight in a metaphysical sense, i.e., does not take it to be the understanding and image of being itself.

What is man primarily? He is, first, the animal capable of symbols (language); second, the one able to use tools; third, a creature with a brain, i.e., the being that uses a far greater proportion of its energy in its brain, especially in the cortex, than do animals.

Symbols, words, so-called concepts, are only *tools*, refined psychological tools. Man has nothing organological, morphological, or physiological, nothing psychic or noetic, which cannot be found incipient in the higher vertebrates. Therefore, descent of man from animals is to be assumed, regardless of scientific debates concerning intermediate forms between Dubois man and documented diluvial man.

Since the Greek sensualism of Democritus and Epicurus, this picture of *homo faber* has been slowly elaborated by powerful trends of positive thought. Bacon, Hume, Mill, Comte, Spencer, later, especially, the theory of evolution associated with Darwin and Lamarck, later still, the pragmatic-conventional (also fictionalist, *as if*) philosophies. Their individual differences do not interest us here. The idea found the support of the great analysts of human drives. Hobbes and Machiavelli can be called their ancestors or, at least, the precursors of one of their orientations. I single out among them Ludwig Feuerbach, Schopenhauer, Nietzsche, and, in most recent times, Sigmund Freud and Alfred Adler.[8] A truly advanced theory of drives is the present objective of Paul Schilder, McDougall, also of Franz Oppenheimer (although he is none too original) and the author. It is conceived as the common philosophical foundation for anthropology and vitalistic psychology, but it is no less basic for sociology and psychotherapy. It will win the definitive victory over that erroneous so-called dualism of body and (vitalistic) soul. This dualism has led anthropology astray ever since Descartes, for, as he failed to see, every sensation, perception, as well as every process of physiological functions, depends on drives. They are precisely what constitutes the *unity* of the psychophysical organism.[9]

A more developed theory of drives and of their manifestations arrives at a very important classification of basic drives. These categories are distinct from those identified by the objectives of drives (egoism proper, altruistic urges favoring others, drives of self-preservation, self-manifestation, of preserving or developing the species, furthermore, individual and collective drives, those of groups, of the herd, etc.). The manifold directions and impulses of drives arise, partly from mere psychoenergetic reactions among the drives which are in continuous opposition to each other, partly, in men, also from the intellectual exploitation of these driving urges. They can be reduced to three, and only three, basic drives. These are: first, the urge to reproduce and all its implications (sexual urge, drive to care for the litter, libido); second, drives for growth and power; third, the drives to nourish oneself, in the widest acceptation of the term. This is not the place to show how closely these three drives are related to the three germ layers of vertebrates, and certainly not the place to show how we can derive them from the complex system of drives in higher animals and in primitive man (the so-called "needs," furthermore the "passions," and "interests").

The question—how fundamental are these drives genetically and what is their relative importance?—has been answered quite differently by the major theories of drives. All growth which is more than increase in size, and which the famous pathologist Friedrich Kraus calls the will to power *katexochen* [supreme], rests upon intra-individual reproduction (division of cells). Also, a cell cannot be nourished without the urge for growth which is its fundamental principle. Besides, plants possess a system of reproduction and nourishment, but, unlike animals, they lack a system of power which delineates them even more sharply from the environment. For these reasons, the author believes that of the three types of basic drives in animals and man, reproduction plays the primary role, power the second, nourishment the third. The psychological analysis of drives during maturation confirms this assumption.

Let us point out one thing. There are three anthropologists who base their theories exclusively on drives. This author rejects them philosophically as "naturalists," but honors them as original scholars in the theory of drives. They are either historically responsible for, or, at least, in logical agreement with, *three* particular *naturalistic philosophies of history*. If we emphasize that man is exclusively a creature of drives and if we derive his so-called mind genetically from drive and perception, e.g., from "repression" and "sublimation," the three naturalistic philosophies of history, which correspond to this naturalistic idea of man, can assume *three* basic forms. These depend on which of the three above mentioned types of drives is accorded the major role.

(1) In the so-called *economic* (Marxist) philosophy of history, history is primarily class struggle and "fight for the feeding place." It finds the most powerful and decisive force, productive of collective action, to be the *drive for nourishment,* and looks upon spiritual and cultural contexts of all kinds as mere epiphenomena and complex detours to satisfying this drive in the changing situations of society in history.

(2) Another naturalistic philosophy of history finds the significant variable of all development in the *mixing* and *purifying of blood,* as well as in the cycles of reproduction and procreation. Among others, Gobineau, Ratzenhofer, and particularly Gumplowicz are representative. This kind of naturalistic philosophy of history corresponds to the theory of drives which sees the *primum movens* [spring] of history in the basic drive to perpetuate the species and in its qualitative and quantitaive manifestations (Schopenhauer, Freud).

(3) The ideology of *power politics* must be called the third type of naturalistic philosophy of history. Taking up the early views of Thomas Hobbes and Machiavelli, it examines the outcome of the struggle for political (thus not economic) power, i.e., the struggles between states for supremacy and those of classes and groups within the states. These conflicts become the decisive factors which determine the possible basic patterns of economic, spiritual, cultural being and events, i.e., they become the basic determinants of history. This philosophy of history corresponds to a theory of man which, like that of Nietzsche and also Alfred Adler, sees the primary motivation of drives in the "will to power" and the struggle for "recognition," i.e., for spiritualized power. This is not the place to show how this specifically political philosophy of history becomes mixed with religious conceptions of history, as in conservative

Lutheranism, with pure naturalism (Thomas Hobbes, Machiavelli, Ottokar Lorenz), or with ideological theories of history, as in Ludwig von Ranke who associates this philosophy with his theory of ideas, or the way it becomes less universal and almost a system of political propaganda, as in Heinrich von Treitschke and the historians who, after the era of Bismarck, advocated the smaller Germany.

These conscious or semi-conscious naturalistic theories of history unfold very different pictures of man's past. We have, for instance, the view of Auguste Comte at the end of the age of enlightenment. His law of three stages was the first to divide the past into epochs of human knowledge and technical civilization and to evaluate them. Comte was tremendously naïve in measuring them by the progress of our modern experimental and inductive sciences, of western European industrialism, and by its scale of values limited in space and time. Thus, he was ready to consider that religion, as well as metaphysics, was an outdated phase of the human spirit.[10] Herbert Spencer's conception of history resembles that of Comte. Conversely, we have the views of Karl Marx and of the historians dedicated to theories of race or those studying political power in government. All these varieties of naturalistic anthropology and historical philosophy have one common characteristic, peculiar not only to them but to conceptions of history which are very different in other respects: the belief, more or less pronounced, that *history forms a great unity,* and the more or less pronounced faith in a *meaningful evolution,* an inescapable movement of history toward *one* great and noble objective. This applies to Kant, Hegel, Ranke (who compromises his position considerably, e.g., in his discourses for King Max of Bavaria, but, after all, maintains his European and liberal orientation), to Comte, Spencer, Darwin, Haeckel, Marx, and Gumplowicz, and to the purely political historians of the school of the smaller Germany, after the era of Bismarck. Only Gobineau is different. They have a common, powerful faith in some kind of evolution of human values, indeed, of man himself, even though they emphasize different aspects and values. They share this faith, often in spite of themselves, and, almost more frequently, against their better judgment. This is what ties them, in a strangely mystical way, to the historical theories of Christian, rationalistic, and humanitarian anthropology. Only Schopenhauer—here Schelling was partly his precursor—honestly does not possess this faith. He is the first complete and exclusive *déserteur de l'Europe* [deserter of Europe] and of the European belief in history. His famous motto is: *"Semper idem, sed aliter"* [always the same thing, but differently], and he was first to demand a merely stationary "morphology of cultures." [11]

IV

The *fourth* of the five ideas about man which rule our epoch contributes a sharply discordant note to this admirable *unisono* [harmony] of modern Occidental anthropology and historical theory. I would like to start by saying that the world of culture in general has neither understood nor recognized the unity, significance, and relative justification of this fourth idea. It is a divergent and strange idea, but one with extensive historical antecedents. One might say that it is frightening for all traditional Occidental feeling and thought. But this frightening idea—could nevertheless be true! That is why we take account of it as it behooves a philosopher.

The radical characteristic of this new anthropology and theory of history is its assumption of the necessary *decadence* of man in the course of his so-called ten thousand years of history, a decadence which it considers inherent in the very nature and origin of man. This is in clear opposition, in the Occident, to all common beliefs of traditional anthropology and historical theory concerning the progressing *"homo sapiens"* or *"homo faber,"* or the "Adam" of Christendom, fallen but again rising and saved in the middle of time, or the creature of drives (the three kinds of basic drives) which, in diverse ways, purifies itself to become a "spiritual being." To the simple question, "what kind of a thing is man?" this anthropology gives the answer: Man's capabilities (use of speech, tools, etc.) are mere substitutes for really vital qualities and activities, which could be developed. In view of this, man is a complete *deserter from life*, its fundamental values, laws, its holy cosmic sense, and lives on a diseased exaggeration of his ego.

Not the certainly profound spiritual fathers, but Theodor Lessing, the adroit publicist of this idea, tried to appeal to those hard to convince and patterned the new theory into this formula: "Man is a species of predatory ape that gradually went mad with pride over its so-called 'mind'." The Dutch anatomist Louis Bolk, the author of excellent studies of the evolution of human organs from such animal ancestors, more appropriately summed up the results of his investigation in the sentence: "Man is an infantile ape with deranged inner secretions." [12] In a similar way, the Berlin physician Paul Alsberg claims to have discovered a "principle of humanity," not concerned with morphological comparison, in the "principle of degenerating organic functions." [13] Strongly influenced by Schopenhauer, the argument runs like this: Man stands quite defenseless in his environment, altogether far less adapted to it than his closest animal relatives. Unable to further develop his organic functions, man has, therefore, developed a tendency to use as few organic functions as possible and to replace them by tools (language and conceptualization are judged to be "immaterial tools") which make it unnecessary to develop functions and sharpen the sensory organs. According to this theory, intelligence is not an a priori spiritual power requiring this disuse and making it possible, but, rather, the result of the fundamental refusal to use these organic functions, indeed, one of the modes of Schopenhauer's "negation of life by the will." [14]

Thus, according to this theory, man, first of all, is not, like some species of plants or animals, some dead-end road of evolution in which life can no longer evolve in a chosen direction and where the species therefore dies. Man is *the* dead-end road to life altogether! Secondly, man is by no means *in genere* [generically] feeble-minded (only few men are that), but his so-called mind itself, his so-called *ratio,* is a disease, a diseased basic trend of universal life itself. This *ratio* is precisely the aspect which, according to Aristotle, Descartes, Kant, and Hegel, makes him into *"homo sapiens"* and partly divine, and, also, the aspect which constitutes his particular "intellectualization," i.e., the fact that so great an amount of accumulated energy is spent, not for the whole of his organized self, but solely for his cerebrum and its maintenance ("slave of the cortex"). The individual is not sick. Within the order of his species, he can even be healthy, but man *himself* is a disease. In our mighty universe, life is possible in only a very few instances, and man could exist only during an infinitesimal portion of the history of life on earth. Thus, the earthworm called man remains the dead-end, the disease of life, even if he acts important and feels that his history has become so important that he creates states, works of art, sciences, tools, language, poetry, etc., so important that he becomes conscious of himself and no longer turns ecstatically to his environment like the animal. Why does he embark on such strange leaps and detours? Proudly and sovereignly Descartes states: *"Cogito ergo sum."* But Descartes, *why* do you think? Why do you have a will? You think because neither your instinct, nor your technical intelligence, which is determined by drives and has objectives remaining within the framework of your drives, directly whispers to you what to do and how to act! You do not think, as you believe, in order to elevate yourself above the animal into new spheres of being or value, but in order to be "more animal-like than any animal"! What do you call "free choice"? You give this name to your frequent hesitations, i.e., to your ignorance of where to go and why to act. The animal always knows these things immediately and without doubt, therefore, better than you! What are sciences, *ratio,* art; what is the higher development of your so-called civilization (machines), which you desire on account of your fertility and which, of course, makes it possible for an even greater number of men to live on the same plot of ground? What is all that, seen as *a whole?* Indeed, it is but a very complex *detour* to your difficult task of maintaining the species, which becomes harder all the time, in spite of your efforts to reproduce, precisely as you think more and become more intellectual. To what purpose do you possess language, insignificant man? Why do you have concepts? Why do you assimilate the many modulated images, suspended in the mind, into identical, fictional objects? Why have you invented unchanging tools for definite purposes? Why have you, in your history, replaced the purely biological leadership of elders, of fathers, the associations of clans which antedate the states, by the state, i.e., by organized rule? Why have you adopted consciously formulated "law" in place of the custom and "tradition" of an unselfconscious people? And why have you, in the monarchic super-state, simultaneously invented the ideas of monotheism and original sin (both belong together)? [15] I will tell you, insignificant man, without concern for your inflated ego. Insignificant man, you did all this, and much more, out of nothing but your *biological weakness and impotence* and out of your fatal lack of biological development. All these actions are the sad surrogates of a life which you could not develop further, nor live beyond your own self! This "no" to life, drives, sense perception, instinct, all this negation which is your very essence as a so-called *homo sapiens,* in control of his will, all this stems from your inability to constitute, with the normal functions of life and in accordance with *its* principles of development, a living being that transcends you, that might be *more than a superman!* As man, this is the principle of your being!

This strange theory, briefly indicated in key concepts, is a rigorously logical conclusion of this argument: In the manner of the theory of *"homo sapiens,"* let us distinguish spirit, or reason, from life, as two ultimate metaphysical forces. Now let us, unlike the argument of *"homo sapiens,"* identify life and soul, spirit and technical intelligence, while, at the same time, and this is decisive, taking the values of life as the highest. In this case, spirit and conscious reason will logically appear as the principle which destroys and even annihilates life, the highest of values. Thus, the spirit is a demon, indeed, the devil, *the* power destructive of life and soul. Spirit and life, accordingly, are not two ultimate and interdependent principles of being, as one might assume because human life and drives are the agents realizing spiritual ideas and values, while the human spirit is the ideational factor giving life its direction and aim. On the contrary, spirit and life appear as two quite antagonistic and even hostile forces.[16] The spirit appears here like a metaphysical parasite which bores its way into life and soul in order to destroy them.

According to this terrifying *pan-romanticism* of a radically vitalistic theory of values, the ten thousand years of our so-called "world history" themselves are identical with this gradual process of destruction. Accordingly, the history of man is only the necessary decline of a *species* which was deathly sick from the start and was born deathly sick, a species which in its very origins, at least in the form of *homo sapiens,* of typical Occidental man, was a *faux pas of life.* The fact that this pathogenic ("spirit born to suffer pain") process, leading to certain death, has already lasted ten thousand years, does not disprove this theory! In comparing the history of a species with that of an individual, ten thousand years are indeed less than the week it takes a patient to die peacefully from disease! The phases of this declining way of life, of this dead-end road, of this disease of life, called man, are structurally identical with the normal stages of aging and death. The life force is progressively overcome by the inner law of the process which the organism has released while aging. Humanity is, so to speak, progressively caught in this process which will stifle it more and more. It is its own world of civilization which, piece by piece, outgrows the strength and force of its own will and spirit, and becomes ever less controllable and follows ever more independent principles. The progression of man from expressing his soul toward attaining a purpose, from dependence on drives to conscious will, from associative living to society (Tönnies), from a corresponding "organic" to a "mechanistic" view of life, from symbol to concept, from the order of clans in the community to the war-like state and to class division, from maternal *chthonic* [earth] religions to the spiritual religion centered on a founder, from magic to experimental technology, from a metaphysics of symbols to experimental science—these are, according to this theory, inevitable phases on the road to certain death. Different cultures may accomplish this process at different times, but the term of humanity as a whole has been set in the not too distant future.

According to this theory, man has lost more than he has gained, not only with respect to his being and existence, but also in metaphysical insight. The "Dionysian" man of drives stands closer to metaphysical reality and appears here as an ideal strongly opposed to the Greek invention of *"homo sapiens,"* the "Apollonian" man. In other words, Dionysian man, with special techniques, excludes the influence of the spirit, that demon, usurper, and despot of life, in order to feel himself part of the great force of life, to regain his lost unity with it. He is the man who carries in him the "images" of the world.

We shall not develop this presentation any further. This theory is surely false, but it is supported by good reasons, as well founded as those supporting positivistic and ideological theories. Let us just add a few facts about its origin in the history of ideas. Its older godfathers are Savigny and the later (Heidelberg) school of romanticism. It was far more distinctly delineated by Bachofen, who, today, again exerts such strong influence.[17] Other godfathers are Schopenhauer, with his intuitive metaphysics of the will, although, of course, with an anti-Dionysian, Indian, and Christian pessimistic appraisal of the power of will; Nietzsche, whose "Dionysian pessimism" (*"ipsissimum"*), especially in his third period, effected the revaluation of the life force into a positive force; in certain respects, also Henri Bergson, and, in some of its aspects, also the modern trends of psychoanalysis.

However, this old romanticism and these ideas of the "godfathers" would never have constituted a fundamentally new anthropology and historical theory if persons of our present epoch had not originally re-created these ideas out of their own life experience and through independent research. Is not that old romanticism childishly simple in its veneration for the Middle Ages? This vitalistic *pan-romanticism,* after all, would prefer to return beyond *homo sapiens* and the diluvial age! Now, it is most notable, that scholars of very different origin and representatives of widely different disciplines arrived at similar results quite independently from each other. Of these investigators, I cite Ludwig Klages, the real philosopher and psychologist of this anthropological trend; Edgar Dacqué, its paleographer and geologist; Leo Frobenius, its ethnologist; Oswald Spengler, its historian; and Theodor Lessing;[18] finally, also, the so-called fictionalistic theory of knowledge of Hans Vaihinger, who laid some of the foundations for the new panromantic anthropology. According to Vaihinger, man, in his spiritual aspects, is primarily the "animal creating useful fictions of life." The theory of objects of Ludwig Klages, e.g., agrees with Vaihinger in its logical content, not in its evaluation.

If one compares this new theory of man, up to now essentially limited to Germany, with the Christian-theological, the rationalist-humanistic *("homo sapiens"),* and the positivistic theories of drives, similarities and differences appear which are not without interest to our discussion.

Dionysians must sharply reject all spiritual and spiritualistic religions, including the Jewish and Christian faiths, and the spiritual God of creation, e.g., because, for the Dionysian philosophers, spirit is precisely the demon destructive of life and the soul. In spite of this, they again approach Christian anthropology with their idea of the fall of man, especially in the form we find in Saint Augustine, with this difference, that for Dionysians no already existing *"homo"* fell or "took" a fall, but that *homo "sapiens" himself is* fall, guilt, and sin. (In a similar way, the older philosophers, Schelling, Schopenhauer, and Eduard von Hartmann, saw the very existence of the world, as differentiated from the ideas realized in it, based on the defection of God's nature from the divine spirit, in other words, based on original sin inherent in the blind yearning for existence.) Conversely, this new anthropology shares with rationalistic anthropology the sharp distinction between life and spirit, taken ontologically. According to Klages, as well as for Aristotle, Kant, or Hegel, the "one" spirit active in all men cannot be understood in terms of natural, psychological, and gradual development. The spirit is of metaphysical origin and not, as positivists and naturalists believe, of empirical nature. It is, therefore, not merely a "sublimated super-structure for animal life." However, and here lies the source of error in this theory, the concept, spirit, is so formulated that it really includes nothing but the mediate thought which characterizes technical intelligence, in the same manner as for positivists and pragmatists. This spirit cannot grasp the realm of ideas and values which are ontological and are valid ontologically. Its objects are only *"ficta"* [fictions] which reflect man. In the senseless rush to capture them, man progressively loses his soul, the hidden womb of his own being. Here the theory remains quite dependent on its real opponent, positive pragmatic anthropology. Secretly, it *follows* pragmatism by pursuing it.* In this Dionysian theory, the spirit, as Logos, cannot open a new realm of being to man, nor can it, as pure love, open a realm of values. It merely provides increasingly complex means and mechanisms for drives. Thereby, it spoils them and destroys their natural harmony. To this we must add: Vitalistic romanticism transformed the spirit from a divinely creative and constructive principle into a demonic, metaphysical power, hostile to life and even to existence.[19] This is diametrically opposed to the true positivism of Comte and Spencer, who honor *homo faber,* while here, as Klages and Lessing so graphically relate, *"homo faber,"* animal of symbol and tools, is the dangerous beast that devastated the world. Like the psychologists of drives, and like the three naturalistic philosophies of history, corresponding to the different theories of drives, this new anthropology, in turn, attaches tremendous importance to the emotional-automatic life of drives and to its unconscious expressions. In opposition to the other theories, however, it ascribes to the emotional life of

* A pun is involved between *folgt* ("follows") and *verfolgt* ("pursues"). *Translator's note.*

drives a metaphysical cognitive function[20] which is, of course, the
only possible one, as long as *ratio* can produce only "ficta" and
empty "indications" concerning life and concepts.

V

And now the last, the *fifth,* of the ideas about man, advanced
today! A particular conception of history parallels it also. This idea
has been little known until now, perhaps even less than the idea just
discussed.

The idea of man we have just explained humiliates man or, at
least, *"homo sapiens,"* identified through almost all of the Occidental
history of ideas with man *in general.* Indeed, it humiliates him more
than any previous theory in history, by calling him "the animal sick
in spirit." The fifth idea, on the contrary, lets human consciousness
of self rise to such a degree, to such a precipitous, proud, and dizzy
height, also, as no other known theory had ever done. The emotional
point of departure of this theory is "the disgust and the painful feeling of shame" which, in Nietzsche's *Zarathustra,* qualify man. Man
can, however, become identified with these feelings only if he is measured by the shining figure of superman, responsible and glad to assume responsibility, lord, creator, meaning of the earth, and sole
justification of what one calls humanity and people, history and the
course of events; indeed, the culmination of being itself. This new
form of anthropology has again taken up Nietzsche's *idea of superman*
and has given it a new rational foundation. This is done in rigorously
philosophical context, particularly by two philosophers who merit
recognition, Dietrich Heinrich Kerler and Nicolai Hartmann, whose
magnificent and profound *Ethik* represents the most rigorous and the
purest philosophical application of the idea.[21]

Kerler, as well as Hartmann, introduces a new kind of atheism
which cannot be compared to any atheism in the Occidental world
before Nietzsche, and which constitutes the basis of this new idea

about man. I usually call it *"postulating atheism of seriousness and responsibility."* What does this mean? In all past atheism (in the widest sense) of materialists, positivists, and others, the existence of God was deemed *desirable* in itself, but, either could not be proved, was directly or indirectly beyond comprehension, or could be refuted by the course of events. Kant, who thought he had refuted all proofs of God, nevertheless considered the existence of an object corresponding to the rational idea, "God," a "generally valid postulate of practical reason." On the contrary, this *new* theory states: It may be true, in a theoretical sense, that something like a source of all things exists, an *ens a se* [thing by itself]. Whether theistic or pantheistic, rational or irrational, in any case we have no knowledge of this unknown object. However, quite apart from whether we know it or not, the following argument is decisive: A God *must* not, and *shall not,* exist for the sake of man's responsibility, freedom, mission, and in order to give meaning to human existence. Nietzsche wrote the following words, so rarely understood: "If there were gods, how could I stand not being a god. Therefore, there are no gods." Here we find the first sharp pronouncement of postulating atheism, the extreme opposite of the postulating theism of Kant. In chapter 21 of Nicolai Hartmann's *Ethik,* entitled "Teleology of Values and Metaphysics of Man," this "postulating atheism of responsibility" is carried to its ultimate conclusion. He tries to give it a rigorously scientific foundation and says: The free, moral being, the "person," can *only* exist in a mechanistic world or, at least, in one which is not teleologically constructed. As a moral being, as a person, man is annihilated in a world created by a divinity according to its plan, or a world in which a divinity, outside of man, has means of controlling the future. "One must choose either a teleology of nature and of being in general, or a teleology of man" (p. 185). Or again: If the world is, in some way, of the same nature as man (and this, Hartmann believes, is the assumption of all past conceptions of divinity), man loses his unique place in the cosmos and his rights. He loses them, not through any causal determinism, nor because of the mechanistic structure of the world. On the contrary, the mechanism gives him the means to transmute into reality what he has discovered in the purely objective order of ideas and values of ideal being. Indeed, the mechanism is the instrument of his freedom and of his sovereign and responsible decisions. However, all predetermination of the future, governed by a being outside of himself, destroys man as such. Heinrich Kerler once expressed this idea even more daringly (in a letter to this author): "What does a source of the world matter to me if, as a moral being, I know, clearly and without doubt, what is good and how I must act. If there is a source of the world and if it coincides with what I consider good, I shall honor it as my friend. If it does not coincide with it, I shall spit on it, even if it crushes me and my purpose as an existing being."

Let us note well: In this form of "postulating atheism," the negation of God is certainly not felt to be a release from responsibility or a lessening of man's independence and freedom, but precisely the greatest imaginable *increase of responsibility and sovereignty*. Nietzsche was the first to think through the consequences, not only halfway, but completely to the end. He not only thought, but experienced, in the depth of his heart, the consequences of the proposition, "God is dead." He can only be dead as long as the superman lives, one who is, so to say, the supergod, the sole justification of the dead God. Hartmann, also, says: "The predicates of God (predetermination and providence) are to be referred back to man." But of course not, as in Comte, to *humanité*, to "the greater being," but to the *person*, i.e., *the* person who possesses the maximum desire for responsibility, fullness, purity, insight, and power. Humanity, people, the history of the great collective entities—all these are but detours to the intrinsic value and radiance of this kind of person. The full reverence, love, and adoration, which men once expended on God and on their gods, are due, then, to this kind of person. In icy solitude and absolute self-reliance, not a derivative being, the person stands, in Hartmann as in Kerler, between the two orders, the realm of mechanistic reality, and the realm of an objective order of values and ideas, freely suspended in itself, and not posited by any living, spiritual Logos. In order to set the direction, meaning, and value of world history, man must not, in thought and will, rely on outside forces. Nothing must control him, neither a divinity that communicates to him what to do and what not to do, nor threadbare bits of thought taken from the old metaphysics of God, such as the concepts, "development" or "tendency to progress" in the world or in history, nor even some collective entity of will.

What does history mean to this anthropology? Kurt Breysig has attempted to answer this question in his recent work on historiography.[22] Even if one considers his answer erroneous (as does this author), one must say, in recognition, that here the historical and categorical personalism of being and values has been considerably deepened. Collective forces in history are not simply denied as, e.g., by Treitschke and Carlyle ("men make history"), but recognized. Still, they are always reduced again to *personal causality*. The actual effect of such an anthropology on historical writing proper is most clearly illustrated by the members of the circle around Stefan George who concern themselves with historical questions. The best examples are the works of Friedrich Gundolf on Shakespeare, Goethe, Caesar, George, Hölderlin, and Kleist.

History, based on this anthropology, becomes a monumental presentation of the "spiritual figure" of heroes and geniuses, or, to adopt Nietzsche's terms, of the "highest examples" of the human species.

V   Man in the Era of Adjustment

The German Institute for Politics does not limit itself to those objectives which characterize such institutions in all lands, to teach scientifically accurate and sober knowledge of all the realities in our society of nations which are pertinent to the policy of state. It has *two* further objectives and justifications for existence, which are rooted in the historic nature and the historic position of our nation: First, it must contribute with all it has and can offer toward overcoming the ancient and tragic German *opposition between power and spirit* which our new and democratic republic has intensified rather than diminished. Second, it must and can help to bring to light the institution which, by its presence or absence, will, I am firmly convinced, decide the fate of this state, a growing German *elite* that can, through its spirit and will derived from the profundities of German history, slowly penetrate and unobtrusively direct our political leadership in all areas. Not a copy, but the *rebirth* of the German spirit, this elite will be wide awake to the contemporary world and to the requirements of the hour.

One can commit no greater error than to consider *democracy and elite* as mutually exclusive concepts. Unfortunately, partisans of this form of government, who are friendly to elites, do so just as frequently as their opponents, whether monarchists or adherents of some form of dictatorship. Pareto, one of the outstanding experts in the matter of elites, said quite correctly not only that history is a "circulation of elites," but that this is true regardless of the form of government under which men live. We know that democracy more ruthlessly *reveals* the existence of historical contrasts between population groups, confessions, classes, and parties in a nation, but that it does not produce them; and by revealing them, it sharply and clearly out-

NOTE: Address given on the anniversary of the Deutsche Hochschule für Politik [German Institute for Politics] in Berlin on November 5, 1927.

lines the future *problems* which the elite has to solve. For very profound reasons which we cannot discuss here, it is, of course, also true that parliamentary democracy in almost the entire world today faces a dangerous crisis. It has a difficult struggle not, as formerly, against conservative legitimists of some sort (today this opposition is almost dead), but against tendencies toward dictatorship on the right and on the left. Democracy will be able to survive only if it can, so to speak, seize the weapons from its opponents and produce and tolerate a well-chosen, mobile, effective elite which provides the nation with a *unity of culture and power.* Whether we Germans will succeed in this task or not, will determine not only the fate of our national culture and the dignity of our human form, but also the historical destiny of our state.

I could not begin to discuss the general, great, sociological problem of historical *elites,* their types, formation, maintenance, spread, and collapse, not even if I limited myself to our country. It is a sociological problem of the greatest importance and, perhaps, particularly worthy of being considered by this Institute. One thing is certain: The elite will *not* be an elite of mere blood and tradition like the old Prussian aristocracy and the caste of state employees which it sponsored. The tasks of our epoch call for human qualities and abilities unlikely to be transmitted from father to son by the principles of psychic inheritance. Nor will the elite arise from one of our all too numerous political parties which have such strong ideological orientations and are so inclined to saw off the limb on which they sit, i.e., by ignoring the measure of *unity* in our national culture and in our conception of German history, without which free democratic discussion and formulation of opinions are impossible in a parliament (we see these difficulties again in the still unfinished fight for the law on public schools). If for no other reason, this will not occur because even specifically political elites—think of that noble elite which arose under the impulse of the War of Liberation [in 1813]—hardly ever grow directly out of the political sphere, but are born in movements which are *spiritually* new and, at the same time, are impelled by a new feeling of *vitality*, and because only then do they slowly enter the political domain. Thus, the Fascist movement grew out of a movement for national rebirth among war veterans and Italian youth. Elites arise no more easily from particular classes nor from definite professions.

At times, some elites have the important function of maintaining and administering particular cultural attainments. However, those elites which time itself exhorts with the word, "create," must ripen in the mysterious depths of the nation and come to light slowly. Above all, they must not be premature in manifesting themselves. They can hardly arise except through the gradual amalgamation of "cultural groups" which have formed around leading personalities. It is my firm belief, derived from years of experience and observation, that such elites are in the early stages of development today, under our new form of government which, in the beginning, was so little adapted to the German people. It may be years yet, perhaps decades, before this growing elite, which today is still too *critical* of our culture, will be prepared for reality and life, able to become effective in our political arena also, and able to replace the present interim leadership in Germany. This rebirth will, however, come not to destroy what our fathers have built at Weimar, but to instill into this emergency framework the ideal of *arete* [virtue] and a *live, spiritual content*.

One condition of forming such an elite, a condition that can be considered even today, is that we should, in as far as possible, acquire a common *conception* of the *structure of the era* we have entered and, at the same time, of the manner in which to refashion the *type* of leader appropriate to this era. I say "era," and not merely age, purposely, for the import of this profound transformation of environment and man, which is beginning today, can hardly be overestimated. Compared with the divisions which historians establish in the life and times of what they call the "modern European period," this change seems even more infinitely profound and varied than the fundamental transformation which leads from the so-called European

Middle Ages to modern times. We must go back to the origins of Christianity and to the rise of the Germanic-Romanic society of nations to find an approximate equivalent of such a profound change. It is not only a transformation of things, circumstances, institutions, of the basic concepts and forms of art, and of almost all other disciplines; it is a *transformation of man himself,* of the nature of his internal constitution in body, drives, soul, and spirit. It is not only a change in his actual being, but in his standards of judgment. The following comment of one of the leaders of German youth is touching in its awkwardness: "We carry in us an [ideal] image of man, but it is such that it cannot serve as our model. However, since we carry it in us, it becomes ever more visible in that the individual reveals it in the freedom of his inner growth."

Especially in times of profound change, all deeper human aspirations, all politics also, are supported, consciously or unconsciously, by such a mysterious, I should say, eschatological, image or ideal of man. Friedrich Nietzsche, the last German genius to consciously try to create such an image and to tie it closely to the idea of a new European elite, called this image of his longing *"superman."* Even if this image has, in a way, powerfully affected all Europe and countries beyond—I call to mind only Mussolini and Fascism—it suffers not only from the unworldly and unreal vagueness of almost all the statements of this great and lonely poet and thinker, but it traversed, in its own development, a number of profoundly different phases which I cannot describe here. Its first and altogether eschatological form was the idea of a new *kind* of man in the biological sense. Its last form was the conception of consciously raising and educating a new historical *elite* within existing species. Nietzsche cites many examples of this from past history, but adds that these represented "only chance and fortunate accident." In this last phase, in which Nietzsche's critique of Darwin and of the general theory of evolution (in many ways, this critique is valuable even today) becomes most pointed, superman is only the conceptualized symbol for establishing the "new tables of value" which resulted from his powerful critique of traditional historical "codes of ethics." I cannot begin to criticize the content of this image. I would like to say only this: As startling as this image may have been, it does *not* seem one which the growing elite of our times can accept as its eschatology of man.

We must completely abandon all thought of an essential transformation of man in the *biological,* especially in the morphological, sense. The entire teaching of scientific biology contradicts the possibility of such a transformation, and supports the idea (which I cannot elucidate here) that man is definitively *fixed* in his morphology. The fact that the possibility of evolving decreases as species attain a more perfect organization and differentiate themselves (Weismann) prevents us from expecting any further biological evolution of man. In historical times, man has certainly not undergone any essential change in his organization. The differentiation of races is probably an early consequence of self-domestication and culture. The evolution of a specifically human "spirit" and of "intelligence," which man shares with the primates, has so basically and methodically replaced the morphological development of man's physical organs, that even the strongest re-sublimation [see below], and even centuries of it could, at best, maintain the present form of his species, but could not produce forces for a continued organic evolution.

The belief that man can change organically by inheriting functionally acquired characteristics, as Herbert Spencer assumed and considered along with spiritual development, seems erroneous to me. Modern scientific research in heredity rejects this theory. Scientists can still investigate whether acquired "propensities" to develop certain characteristics can be inherited, not, however, as directly and somatically induced in the inheritance-carrying genes of the germ plasm, but only in its protoplasmic structure. The process is, therefore, much more indirect and works over much more extensive periods of time than Spencer assumed. Furthermore, not only the accumulation of actions, but also the development of the spirit and of its forms of activity in man, have become *autonomous* and *independent of his physical organization* and are, therefore, to be studied by "intellectual disciplines" independent of biology. Therefore, when Spencer wants to give biological reasons for growth in psychic and social harmony, in the a priori assets of the human mind, and in the moral sentiments of man; when, to express it in pictorial language, he sees a movement of the species toward the increasingly tame and intellectual herd-animal and toward a so-called "social equilibrium," his expectation of things to come lacks all scientific foundation.

If such a progressive biological evolution of the species and growth of man on earth seem quite improbable, his biological *decadence* is no less so. While the picture of the future drawn by Spencer, Darwin, and Nietzsche was too brilliant, today an image which is equally exaggerated in its gloom appeals to large segments of youth, especially German youth. I am thinking particularly of the picture of the future, also biologically conceived, which Ludwig Klages displays with much imagination and skill. Klages' judgment is characteristic of German late romanticism. His theory of the nature of man sees the "spirit," consciousness, the will, and the ego in history gnawing more and more at "life" and "soul," which contain all the high values of existence. Consequently, to the extent that man "thinks," he *must* think "mechanically," and to the extent that he "wills," he must produce an increasing number of mechanisms and place them between himself and virginal nature, to a point where he can no longer dominate and rule these mechanisms and where they, so to speak, bury him. I named Ludwig Klages as the outstanding exponent of such pan-romanticism. (I could equally well have mentioned Leo Frobenius, Edgar Dacqué, Oswald Spengler, Theodor Lessing.) According to their doctrine, in as far as it is man who technologically dominates organic nature, the road of the spirit is the *road of death* for the life and soul of man as well as for living nature, since the individual being itself psychologically and physiologically produces the mechanisms which cause its death.

How understandable psychologically, at the same time how suggestive for our hearts, is this somber picture of the future of man which seems to indicate only one solution, to take refuge in a remote corner of nature and there mourn for man and his history, admire his distant past and its last remnants in myth, legend, tale, and usage, and to intoxicate oneself, shun all "action," and thus immerse oneself pathologically in the lost days of the original soul! During the World War we used to read in the reports, "for technical reasons it was impossible . . . ," for instance, to cancel the submarine warfare at the decisive moment or, at the outset of the war, for the Tsars to revoke the Russian mobilization, etc. Those of us who lived through this, who experienced all the recent developments of the Occident in the twentieth century in their small and large aspects, the increasing difficulty of controlling the masses, the impossibility of directing capital which has become autonomous—did we not, every one of us, in our own bosoms, experience feelings akin to this somber theory of decadence? But what significance has this late Occidental intermezzo for the whole of *humanity?* It is minor or non-existent! This pessimistic theory is just as narrowly European as positivism which believes in progress, only with inverse values. After all, a European crisis is neither the signal for the death of humanity, nor for the "decline of the West"! This pessimistic attitude may be important as a call to arms, but it does *not* foretell our future. The "spirit" is no enemy of life or of the soul! Of course, it causes wounds, but it also heals them. For instance: Capitalism brought about the devastation of organic nature when man, until the eighteenth century, used wood for heating purposes; in the subsequent period, when heating was done with coke and coal, the same capitalism placed inorganic energy in the service of the economy and thus left organic life protected and safe; and capitalism will, in the future, know how to use sources of energy which transfer the same socially useful tasks to more inferior forces (like waterpower, radio-active energy) in order thus to *liberate* higher ones. Not the spirit, only the over-sublimated *"intellect,"* which Klages confuses with "spirit," the "intellect which lacks wisdom," devoid of elevated *ideas* and values of reason—*it* is, in some measure, the enemy of life! Is *re*-sublimation—I shall explain later what I mean by this—not possible here, using systematic eugenics following the system so meritoriously propagated, in Germany, by Eugen Fischer of the Kaiser Wilhelm Institute, and in many other ways? One more thing: I admit that our limited cultural sphere is in danger of perishing through mechanization; that means not of dying out, but of becoming politically and culturally impotent, but only if no new art of *self*-control comes to the aid of the control *over nature* which the Occident has, up to now, developed so exclusively. We shall consider this later.

Speaking of the future and of a new image of man, I cannot conceive any future image which envisages an automatic transformation, whether positive or negative, of man's organic, natural aptitude, but only one which represents an "ideal" that admits man's *freedom to develop himself,* an ideal implying that man himself will shape that infinitely plastic segment of his nature which can be influenced directly or indirectly by the spirit and the will. What comes from the spirit does not come automatically, nor does it come of itself. It must be guided! In this sense, we accept the word of the Frenchman Gratry: "Not only the individual, but also humanity can end as saint or criminal, depending on how it directs its *will*." Man is a creature whose very essence is the open decision. What does he want to *be* and to *become?*

However, this ideal for man is, if it must have a name, the *"total man,"* not the "superman" conceived separately from the masses and from all democracy. Through the ideal of total man, superman and subman are to become *human.*

In his known history, man has proven himself a being of tremendous *plasticity.* Therefore, the greatest danger for all philosophical attitudes is to conceive the idea of man too *narrowly,* to derive it unintentionally from *one* natural or even historical form, or to see it contained in any such narrow conception. The idea of the *"animal rationale"* in the classic sense was much too restricted. *"Homo faber"* of the positivists, "Dionysian man" of Nietzsche, man as a "disease of life" of the new panromantic doctrines, "superman," *"homo sapiens"* of Linné, *"l'homme machine"* of Lamettrie, man solely as "power," "libido," and "economic" being, in Machiavelli, Freud, and Marx, fallen, God-created Adam—*all* these conceptions are much too narrow to encompass the *whole* of man. Furthermore, all these concepts are like ideas of *things*. But man is not a thing. He is a direction of the *movement of the universe* itself, even of its source. Man is "microcosm and a being filled with spirit." I hope that these definitions are not already too narrow to include his many possibilities and forms. *Allow us, therefore, room for man and for his movement which is infinite by nature, and do not tie man to a "model," to a pattern, whether in natural or in world history!* "Mankind bears in itself an infinite number of developments, more mysterious and larger than one might imagine" (Leopold von Ranke).

Total man, in the absolute sense, is hardly close to us. It is the idea of a man who contains and has realized *all* his essential capabilities. Indeed, he is as far from us as God who, in so far as we grasp his essence in spirit and life, is nothing but the *essentia* [essence] of man, only in infinite form and fullness. However, every age of human history knows a *relatively total man,* a *maximum* of total humanity which is accessible to it, a relative maximum of participation in the highest forms of human existence. This is also true for us.

In order to qualify this relatively total man, accessible today, as our guiding ideal, permit me to start from the idea of the *task for the coming era.*

If I had to inscribe a name on the gate of the incipient era, a name which was to render the inclusive trend of this era, only one would seem appropriate to me, that of *"adjustment";* adjustment of almost all characteristic and specifically *natural* traits, physical and psychic, which distinguish the social groups into which we can divide humanity, and, at the same time, a tremendous *increase* in *spiritual,* individual, and relatively individual, e.g., national differences; adjustment of *racial* tensions; adjustment between mentalities, conceptions of self, world, and God, in the great *cultural groupings* especially in Asia and Europe; adjustment between the specifically *male* and *female* ways of thinking in their rule over human society; adjustment between *capitalism* and *socialism* and, thereby, of class arguments and class conditions and rights between *upper* and *lower classes;* adjustment in the share of political power of so-called *civilized, half civilized,* and *primitive peoples;* adjustment also between relatively primitive and highly civilized mentalities; relative adjustment between *youth* and *old age* in the evaluation of their mental attitudes; adjustment between *technical knowledge* and *cultural growth,* between physical and spiritual labor; adjustment between the spheres of *national economic* interests and the contributions which the *nations* make, in the realm of the *spirit* and civilization, to the total culture and civilization of humanity; finally, adjustment between the one-sided *ideas about the nature of man* of which I have just named several types.

Let us note: This tendency toward adjustment which is accompanied by an ever increasing differentiation of the spiritual individuality of man, this adjustment is not something we "choose"; it is inescapable *fate.* Whoever resists, whoever wishes to cultivate some so-called "characteristic," "specific" ideal of man, one already concretely formed in history, will work in thin air. The modern world is full of attempts to revive all possible forms of the species "man," as if the world were a secondhand shop full of discarded relics, "pagan" man, "early Christian" man, "Gothic" man, "Renaissance" man, "Latin-Catholic" man (France), "mushik" man [Russia], etc. Humanity will silently pass by such artificial romantic aspirations!

As I said, adjustment itself is the *inescapable fate* of mankind which found its first truly common experience in the World War, for it is the beginning of the *one* common history of so-called humanity. Even so, it is the *task of the spirit* to *guide* and *direct* this adjustment of group qualities and forces in such a way that the species will *gain in value* while the adjustment takes place. This is the task of all *politics,* indeed, its primary task.

The last epoch was essentially one of growing tensions which kept becoming more particularized, the epoch of the "growth of forces," as Rudolph Eucken called it. This trend was relatively seldom interrupted by violent revolutionary processes which released tension, such as the Peasant Wars, the English and French revolutions, the little German and the great Russian revolution. However, the most general formula applicable to the incipient era, the era of a *universal relaxation of tensions* in human relations, is, it seems to me, that of the *adjustment* of forces. It is, at the same time, an era in which man once again relies on his living spirit and heart and tries to become the *master* of demonic powers which had become *centers of attention* after being unleashed by the last epoch. His purpose is to make these powers serve the salvation of humanity and the meaningful realization of spiritual values. Every policy intended merely to prevent or hinder this fated adjustment or a portion thereof will be swept away by the powerful, irresistible current toward adjustment, and, today, every *political objective,* conceived in formally correct terms, is, in fact, a task of guiding and directing some phase of this adjustment, so that it may proceed with a minimum of destruction, explosion, blood, and tears.

As I said, this seems to me the most universal formula for any policy in the new era, for we must clearly understand one thing: Not the periods of increasing tension and particularization of forces, but the *periods of adjustment* are the *most dangerous* for humanity, the most filled with death and tears. Every process which we call explosion, catastrophe, in nature and history, is a process of adjustment which is *not* meaningfully led by the spirit and will, or is not amenable to their leadership.

Let us sketch a few *types* of this coming adjustment.

The racial adjustment, the mixing of blood, will progress irresistibly. Immanuel Kant had already predicted that adjustment of racial tension was inevitable. Whoever sees the salvation of the world in the maintenance of a "pure" race, in his opinion a "noble race," can do nothing but imitate the "seven faithful friends" of Count Gobineau; let him withdraw to an island with his pure race, and despair! The rise of independent colored peoples has already made striking progress. An adjustment between white and colored peoples has to come, *but* it can be carried out well or badly, either so that the right kind of blood is mixed, producing higher values according to scientific experience, or so that an inadequate mixture leads to the depreciation of values in the species. Whether one interprets the great racial groups that make up humanity polygenetically and does not believe humanity is racially related, or whether one thinks monophyletically, in any event, the distinction of races was part of the process of *becoming* man. A *united* humanity was not a starting point of history, racially or culturally, but remains its *objective*. In its most formal structure, world history consists neither of a rhythmic unfolding of a plurality of elements, whether the fate of races, or so-called "cultures" which flourish, ripen, and decline near and independently from each other, as Oswald Spengler so suggestively presented it while neglecting all mixtures of race, all reception of foreign ideas and renaissance movements; nor is history one *single* movement, continuous since the beginning and only later separated into different streams through differences in milieu or in historically acquired talent, as is assumed by all specifically Christian and positivistic conceptions of history, both limited in their European view. Instead, the structure of history resembles a river system in which a great number of rivers continue their particular courses for centuries but, nourished by innumerable affluents, finally tend to converge ever more directly and to unite in *one* great stream. The historical currents, which decrease in number, give birth to the historical organisms we call civilizations and cultures. In so far as these stem from the rational *spirit* of the unity of a people, a spirit that, in its structure, is always concretely unique, they are immortal on earth and *outlive* the ethnic unities and their political and economic institutions. Their objective content of meaning and value, which forms the spirit, can, at any time, rise again in renaissance movements and in mixed cultures and form men. Thus, for instance, antiquity was able to fertilize the Occidental world in ever renewed form and manner. However, to the extent that historical organisms are merely "expressions," merely physiognomies of the *soul* and *life* of groups (like legend, fairy tale, myth, usage, custom, etc.), their significance as living values is definitely destroyed and lost when the ethnic unit dies; they are *mortal*. In strong contrast to purely "spiritual culture" and also to "patterns of expression and life of the soul," the collective products of spirit, drive to power, and intelligence, especially experimental science, technology, forms of government and administration, rules of law, in short, the civilizing, not cultural, organisms are the only ones that simultaneously manifest a "progress" continuing beyond national existence, cutting across forms of culture, and also a rectilinear "cumulative effect" that becomes more and more "international." However, "cosmopolitan" adjustment which is the adjustment of purely spiritual forms of culture, not only contemporary ones but those which arose in the past, survive, and are capable of surviving, is incomparably slower and proceeds by very different means than the "international" adjustment of civilization and technology which is linked particularly to world trade and which is, true enough, a prior condition for "cosmopolitan" adjustment.[1]

Among the various kinds of adjustment, a very important one is the cultural adjustment appropriate to the *man himself* of our era, to man who produces and creates all history.

An adjustment which, even today, strikes our attention wherever man, growing into total man, begins to form elites is that between *"Apollonian"* and *"Dionysian"* man, taken as ideas, as species. In the form of "rationalism" and "antirationalism," as "philosophy of ideas" and "philosophy of life," this opposition has, up to now, introduced a dichotomy into the philosophical thought of all nations.[2] This adjustment appears not only in the Occident, but no less in America, as a strange process which is already well under way and scares and even terrifies too many among us who measure only by the standards of the past era. In order to encompass this process with *all* the wealth of the symptoms that we can observe today, I would like to call it a *process of re-sublimation*. By re-sublimation I mean the spiritually conscious act of reducing the amount of accumulated energy which the organism transfers to the brain or to the intellect, the apparent locus of all purely spiritual activity, i.e., of all acts of ideation.

This process of *re*-sublimation first manifests itself only in a *diminished appreciation of the spirit,* especially of intellectuality, of the works of the spirit and its specific social agents. Today, all great modern mass movements in Europe and in America are strangely united in their conscious *antirational, anti-intellectual* attitude which frequently even makes a show of despising the spirit and all spiritual values. The nature and politics of the Soviet Union rest on two elements. They are fed by the fire of anti-intellectual, anti-Western, romantic Pan-Slavism, and supported by the doctrine of western European "Marxism" that spurns ideas. Fascism is specifically vitalistic. Its activist representatives despise scholars and intellectuals. Some time ago, Mussolini said to someone I know: "Here in Italy, they teach the practical application of the birth of tragedy," i.e., of "Dionysian" man. We need only look at the *athletic* movement, growing monstrously in all countries; the *youth* movements with their modern "body consciousness" and appreciation of the body, not only as a source of work and enjoyment, but, in itself, as beauty and form. We see the mighty *eugenic* movement in America; the disappearance of the Puritan ideal of morals, as Ben Lindsey, judge of a juvenile court, describes it in his book *The Revolt of Modern Youth;* the new *erotic* customs of youth in all countries; the great movement of *psychoanalysis* and the *modern psychology of drives;* the rage of dancing all around the world; the *pan-vitalistic* doctrines, newly formed since Nietzsche and Bergson; the strange contemporary propensity toward dark *mysticism*[3] and the very childish despising of science in favor of fraternal or group ideologies; the rapidly decreasing appreciation of the man who is exclusively a scholar, of the intellectual artist, of the intellectual theater; the "heroic types" in contemporary sport or cinema, who have already become almost mythological; the feverish desire for "strength," "beauty," and "youth"; the new appraisal of *infant* existence and of youth as something of intrinsic value; the enjoyment of *primitive,* mystical mentality, art, and spirit; the whole trend to reintroduce into Europe the customs of peoples who were once civilized by Europe, the "countercolonization" of Europe (Moritz Julius Bonn). *All* these circumstances and thousands of others point toward what I would call *a systematic revolt of man's drives in the new era against one-sided sublimation,* against the exaggerated intellectualism of our fathers, their century-old ascetic practices, and their techniques of sublimation (already subconscious) which, up to the present, have fashioned Occidental man. For the time being, the gods of so-called "life" seem to have replaced the rule of the gods of the "spirit"; for I do not consider this movement as a very transitory "post-war phenomenon." It had begun before the war, as the figure of Nietzsche suffices to show; he gave the word "life" its magic sound. In fact, I see a collective movement, deeply rooted in the history of the Occident, aiming at a *redistribution* of man's *total energy* between the cortex and the rest of his organism.

Are these movements so surprising after all? Do they not constitute necessary ways to *health* for modern mankind, even if they first far transgress all boundaries of truth and justice, especially in their ideological expression, as does every typical movement of reaction? Man finds his way to God, as Luther says, only like a drunken peasant, reeling to the right and left. Ever since late antiquity and the appearance of Jesus, ever since the Judaic theistic view began to rule the Occident, the ascetic ideal has developed a most *one-sided* species of man, in ever renewed forms and with completely different causal explanations. Finally, this species began seriously to endanger the equilibrium of human powers. First came the early Christian and patristic asceticism as an antithesis to the paganism of antiquity; then the asceticism of medieval monks and monasteries, relatively harmless since it affected only a small minority; then the progress of this ascetic ideal among the masses and "laymen," not least of all through Protestant asceticism, the "advocates of the inner world," as Max Weber and Ernst Troeltsch called them; and, finally and increasingly, the tremendous capitalistic "asceticism of the golden idol" (Karl Marx), the asceticism of work and industry aiming for unlimited accumulation of products. These forms have, in our culture, led men to a degree of "intellectualization" in their functions or, psychologically speaking, to a "sublimation" which, in the present era, had to turn into a revolution of life and drives if the human equilibrium was to be re-established. The *revolt of nature in man had to* come some day, the revolt of all that is dark, impulsive, and instinctive, of the child against the grownup, the wife against her husband, the masses against the established elites, of the colored against the whites, of what is unconscious against the conscious, of circumstances themselves against man and his intellect! Not in its purely political causes, of course, but in the attitudes of the masses toward it, the World War itself was a *result* rather than a cause of this repression of drives and of this incipient revolt of the drives against the highly intensified, *over*-intensified "Apollonian" and ascetic "rationalism" of the past. The movement, in so far as it concerns the psychophysiological process of *re*-sublimation, is, therefore, neither to be praised nor reprimanded! It represents almost an organic need, although it is, of course, being pursued most onesidedly, but no more so than the unlimited asceticism and spiritualization of the preceding epoch of sublimation.

This is not true for the ideological bubbles produced by the movement, the one-sided philosophies and "religions of life" which are, of course, not justified in pretending to reveal lasting truth. These ideologies forget *two* circumstances: *young,* forceful peoples and men, thirsting for life and still unaccustomed to higher intellectual activity, arrive themselves at *ascetic* ideals and at a higher appreciation of *spiritual* life, and have the urge to sublimate. Thus, the young, forceful, Germanic nations enthusiastically accepted the spiritual Christianity of late antiquity. The *re*-sublimation, however, wherever it appears and in whatever ideas and forms of value it is clothed, is itself a sign of *old age,* of tiring vital functions, just like re-reflection, the yearning, produced by reflection, for the primitive and childlike, for a "second" childhood. It is, of course, also a first systematic attempt to *counteract* and overcome the sublimation in the direction of intellect! Anyone who takes the cry for "life," the whole theoretical and practical "vitalism" of our times, to be the expression of a particular unusual fullness of *life* is being childish. The vitalism of our times is a *counter-ideal,* a *"medicina mentis"* [mental antidote], not an immediate expression of excess strength. Children want to grow, not to remain children. The high value attached to childhood is a product of adults who yearn to be children again!

Quite aside from this, the Occident has for so long sublimated its vital force in a one-sided manner, has tried to banish all expressions of "nature" from man with such insistence, and has cultivated such one-sided, spirit-centered consciousness of self and a feeling for life so infinitely *dualistic,* that even a century of systematic re-sublimation can do no harm. In any event, man is entitled to curtail the asceticism and sublimation of his historical evolution, since he has already spiritualized himself automatically and ontologically. The history of ethics is a story of *loosening* external restrictions as appropriate levels of sublimation and an appropriate force of inner commitment are attained.

Of course, what we see today does not as yet approach even a relative realization of total man. It is only an introduction, the overture to such an evolution. If re-sublimation has succeeded, up to a point, if we again take the vital values to be *self-evident,* those values which modern times, especially the trend of thought since Descartes, have buried under intellectuality and mechanistic attitudes, we have yet to re-establish a new *equilibrium,* so that the spirit and spiritual values will regain the importance befitting the *nature* of man. Only then will we have made a step ahead toward total man, i.e., toward the man of *highest tension between spirit and drive,* idea and sensuality, who is *also* the man with an organized, *harmonious integration* of these two forces into *one* form of existence and one kind of action. Only then shall we have overcome that fatal and even infamous romantic decomposition, that disunity of idea and reality, of thought and action, which is the disease of all intellectual life in Europe and, unfortunately, not least of all in our Germany.

The man who is most deeply rooted in the darkness of earth and nature, and of the *"natura naturans"* which produces all natural phenomena, *"natura naturata,"* the man who, *simultaneously,* as a spiritual person, in his consciousness of self, reaches the utmost heights of the luminous world of ideas, that man is approaching the idea of total man, and, therewith, the idea of the substance of the very source of the world, through a constantly *growing interpenetration of spirit and drive.* "The person who has had the deepest thoughts, loves what is most alive" (Hölderlin).

This movement toward adjustment between spiritual and vital principles in man is paralleled by another, no less significant, the analogous adjustment between *male and female principles* in mankind. The thoroughly terrestrial, earthly, Dionysian phase of our era has a clear tendency toward a new *rise in the value* and *power* of woman. Today we sense it deeply and it will, no doubt, further affect our deepest and ultimate concepts. Since the disappearance of the cult of mother earth, the Occidental concept of God has been influenced ever more one-sidedly by the masculine and logical element. In the framework of the Christian church, Protestantism destroyed the last vestige of the ancient cult of the mother goddess, the cult of Mary as *Theotokos,* as well as the cult of the "mother church." Up to now, the idea of God has been entirely *virile* in conception and feeling. This has been well expressed by H. G. Wells in his book *God, the Invisible King.* (Bismarck, that virile spirit, felt and judged in a similar way, and Soloviev also makes pronouncements to this effect.) As a dogmatic concept, our idea of God seems not to have developed in this direction. I say, it only *seems* that way because, as long as the source of all being is just "pure spirit" and "light," and as long as only a *spiritual* principle is attributed to it, without the attributes of "life" and "drive," this source is *de facto* conceived and expressed, as being and idea, in just as one-sided a

virile, logical way as the classical idea of man as *"homo sapiens."* [4]
Etymologically, in many languages, the term for "human being"
goes back to the word "man." The recent movement toward a new
significance and adoration of woman, a hetaerism rather than a cult
of Demeter [of physical enjoyment rather than of fruitfulness],
toward adjustment between the value of the sexes, though not quite
toward a "matriarchal" law, can be accompanied by excesses of all
kinds. Still, this development is a link in the total process which I
designate as re-sublimation. It will also serve to show the way toward
total man to persons who are exclusively and excessively spiritual
and *over*-sublimated, and who measure everything according to male
standards of value.

A further adjustment of major importance, affecting the formation of man, is that between *Europe* and the three great *Asiatic*
centers, India, China, and Japan, with Islam as an intermediary. It
started long ago and will progress considerably in the future. Here
also, Europe has long ceased to be the only active contributor. Since
Europe has transmitted and continues to transmit the methods of
its technical and economic production, and the sciences on which they
are based, to these Asiatic nations, they become increasingly independent of Europe by developing their own industries. Europe, on
the other hand, and Germany, since Wilhelm von Humboldt, Schelling, and Schopenhauer, absorbs more and more deeply into its
spiritual body the old wisdom of the East, e.g., the ancient Asiatic
technique of living and suffering. This knowledge comes to it through
innumerable channels and, recently, in much greater proportions.
Thus, Europe may succeed in making it its own *living* possession. A
truly cosmopolitan world philosophy is in the making or is, at least,
the basis of a current movement. It not only records for history the
highest axioms of existence and life in Indian philosophy, Buddhist
religion, Chinese and Japanese wisdom, which for so long were
completely unknown to us; it also tests them *objectively and* makes
them into a *vital* element of its own thought. The spiritual modes

established by antiquity, Christianity, and modern science are not being abandoned. Such an attempt would lead in the wrong direction. However, the picture of modern man is being essentially and considerably modified.

Another result is an adjustment of the *ideas* about man and the *models* he emulates. Such an adjustment will have to reconcile, above all, the basic Occidental ideal of the extroverted, *active "hero,"* and the ideal, most widespread in Asia, particularly in early southern Buddhism, of the *suffering "sage"* who meets the pain and evils of existence by his art of suffering, of "non-resistance," or rather by spiritual resistance to the extroverted and automatic reactions to evil. It is characteristic of human nature to annul every pain and evil, from the simplest physical pain to the most profound suffering of the spiritual person, in one of two ways: from *without,* by transforming external irritations that cause it; from *within,* by removing our instinctive resistance to the irritation, in short, by the art of endurance.[5]

We Occidentals lack any *systematic technique for overcoming suffering from within.* We do not believe in such a technique, nor in our ability to keep developing it. This, I firmly believe, is the principal reason for our centuries of fixation on the Judeo-Christian doctrine of the fall of man, of original sin, of suffering imposed as punishment for this, and of the closely related need to save *others* (and of the consequent doctrines of grace and revelation), unknown to the elites of classical antiquity. Until recently, we also lacked psychological techniques, in the sense of systematic psychotherapy and of the art of guiding the inner life and soul. The past century of essentially naturalistic medicine, intent on treating individual organs and cell groups, paid no attention to such methods. But, since the living body and soul are structurally *one,* the entire life process must theoretically be subject to *two* types of influences, to physical, chemical stimuli *and* to those exerted through the corridor of consciousness. Whether and to what extent this is true must be ascertained by experimental science and techniques. These effects can be observed not only in nervous diseases, but in organic and internal diseases of the organism.

Up to the present, there is one thing we have not seriously asked ourselves, the question of whether our whole Western civilization, this one-sided and overactive, *extroverted* process, might not, in the final analysis, be an *attempt to proceed with inadequate means,* judging from the experience of history as a whole, unless this process is accompanied by the contrasting art of winning *inner* power over our whole inferior, non-spiritual, psychophysical "life," which normally operates automatically, an art of meditation, introspection, endurance, and contemplation of being. Might it not be—I propose the extreme case—that the man intent *only* on external power over other men and objects, over nature and body, *without* the above mentioned action and counterbalance of a technique of self-control, would accomplish the *opposite* objective from the one he has in mind, that he might sink into an ever increasing, *slavish dependence* on that mechanism of nature which he himself has read into and placed into nature as the ideal area for his active interference? Bacon said: *"Naturam nisi parendo vincimus"* [we defeat nature only by obeying it]. Is it, however, not equally true that *"naturam paremus, si nil volumus quam naturam vincere"* [we obey nature if we want to do nothing but defeat nature]? An Indian myth tells us of the young God Krishna who, for a long time, had vainly fought in a river with the world snake that was coiled around him. The snake is the symbol of causal relationship in the world. When Krishna's divine father called on him to remember his celestial nature, he escaped the hostile embrace of the snake by adapting his entire body to the coils of the snake, by *giving in* to them completely! The Indian myth adds that he escaped as easily as a lady takes her hand out of a glove. The Judeo-Christian concept of man is altogether *one-sided* and essentially inadequate as compared, for instance, to the Chinese, Indian, and classical Greek ideas of man. In accord with its conception of a creative and working God, unknown to the Greeks, to Plato, and to Aristotle, the Judaeo-Christian idea fixedly opposes man, particularly as lord of creation and creature of power and purpose, to nature. Thus, it *lifts* him *out* of the total structure of life and out of the natural cosmos in a way no other historical idea of man has done. This idea does not become more adequate by being associated with the errors of the "classical" conception of "spontaneous reason" and the "spontaneous power of ideas"!

Man must again learn to grasp the great, invisible, mutual *solidarity of all beings* in total life, of all spirits in the eternal spirit, and, simultaneously, the *solidarity of the world process with the evolution of its first cause* and the solidarity of this cause with the world process. Man must accept this relatedness of the world, not only as a theory, but also live it and practice and activate it externally and internally. God's essence is no more "lord" of the world than man is "lord and king" of creation, but both are, above all, companions of each other's fate, enduring, overcoming, some day perhaps victorious.

The contrast between Eastern and Western approaches to the world, which I have just indicated, also finds special expression in *politics* and political methods. The significance of this effect is generally far underestimated. I mean that profound contrast between "politics of the hunter," positive power politics, and "politics of the victim," negative politics of nonresistance, which is the art of enticing the "hunter" into chaotic spaces, into large areas where the hunter will tend to err and stumble and fail to find a center of force from which he can control the entire area. The terrifying moment in Napoleon's life when Moscow had been set afire by the Russians themselves, as Leopold von Ranke so strikingly described it in his *Erhebung Preussens,* was perhaps the first example of a *kind* of situation which may recur frequently in future conflicts between the positive power politics of European states and the negative political methods of Asiatic countries. This also applies to British politics and capabilities in China, and to the policy of "non-resistance" in which Mahatma Gandhi unites Hindus and Mohammedans against British despotism in India.

If we acquire and perfect special techniques of endurance and suffering and integrate them with the technique of exerting external power, so thoroughly developed in the Occident, we shall be able to effect a *transformation of all knowledge of culture;* I mean, we shall be able to subordinate technical and experimental knowledge of achievement, as well as knowledge of culture, to metaphysical knowledge of grace and salvation.[6] Contemplation of essence, the fundamental approach to being, peculiar to metaphysical knowledge, is principally and necessarily tied to a "passive" and submissive attitude which, at times, *stops* the center of vital drive and its activity. True *"experience"* of nature, as opposed to natural *"science,"* with its objective of controlling nature, also demands an attitude of *loving devotion*. We must again acquire a deep understanding of the "language" of nature, as Francis of Assisi once understood it, or Fabre in his *Souvenirs entymologiques*. We must unlearn the foolish theory that mathematical natural science, admirable as it may be, is the only possible way for us to participate in nature. Goethe's profound insight—"is not the nucleus of nature in the heart of man?", —self-immersion in *"natura naturans"* itself, that inner dynamic cooperation with the great, inclusive process of growth from which every natural organism stems, as it springs from the spirit and drive of eternal substance—all this is something quite different from mathematical science! As Fabre shows, such knowledge from within can produce in individual living creatures not only a general Dionysian participation in vital cosmic being, but also a great Apollonian experience of culture. This knowledge makes man *noble* and happy, while natural science educates him and empowers him to organize and *control* nature. Had man *not* undertaken an inner return to nature, had he *not* acquired a new feeling of oneness with nature, this new love for nature, which manifested itself so powerfully a few years ago in the German and Italian youth movements, then, indeed, the time might have come when man would no longer have cared to control even what, before, he had so exclusively wanted to control and when he would not have considered life worth enough to pursue the specific vitalistic value of having "power over nature"!

Analogous considerations apply to *metaphysics* which has true meaning only if it really penetrates man by constant ideation and by reducing individual fortuitous experiences to their essential aspects. Only in this manner is the self liberated and redeemed from fear, from the pressure of mere "existence," from the fortuitousness of fate; only thus does it become what it was for Plato, Aristotle, Spinoza, and Kant, the *free breath of man* in danger of being stifled by the specific, concrete nature of his "environment." The Occident has almost completely lost the idea of metaphysics and, even more, its technique and method of attaining knowledge. Metaphysics is completely stifled, on the one hand, by the rough dogmatism of the churches and, on the other hand, by experimental and technical knowledge of achievement. To isolate and separate man from his immediate existential environment and contact with life, from the source of all things, means to restrict his horizon terribly, indeed, to choke his inner life; this is just as bad as to cut him off from nature. As Goethe said, man needs *three* objects of veneration, veneration of what is above him, under him, and beside him.

An adjustment must and will take place in this sphere. It is one of the most important *tasks of cultural policy* to guide it in the right direction. Above all, the *cultural task* of our German schools, especially of the advanced institutes, must not be looked upon, as it was in the past, as a merely secondary concern, as something incidental compared with *technological* education. The increasing adjustment between *physical and mental labor* (Rathenau), a generous movement of popular education that fills the soul of the proletariat which had been almost excluded from the spiritual values of the nation—all this is only possible if even the higher classes of society understand the cultural task as a special, separate concern.[7] Mere technical knowledge and methods divide men, but true cultural knowledge permits them to breathe together in *one* spiritual, national realm. A minority of uneducated technicians, superimposed on an unformed mass of laborers, would be civilized barbarism.

These critical forms of future adjustment, which affect the human qualities of new elites, lead us to the adjustment affecting *classes* and *nations*.

The adjustment of *political* and *economic* tensions in Europe is a *fate* imposed by the results of the World War and the changed power structure of the whole continent. The increasing adjustment of tensions in the spheres of political power and economic interests will not in the least threaten the great historic and national cultural entities; it will further stimulate and establish their spiritual and cultural autonomy. Of course, the great historical idea of the nineteenth century, that of the national state, absolutely sovereign and centralized, with an expansive economy and colonial policy, will have to retreat considerably in the coming era. For this reason alone, we Germans have little cause for acquiring new colonies. A certain measure of federalism will be realized in various forms. England has already proceeded most generously with its dominions. One circumstance has been insufficiently noted so far: The *bourgeoisie* and, above all, independent bourgeois entrepreneurs have suffered increasing losses in power and importance, even though the bourgeoisie consisted of *those* classes and groups which were truly responsible for the "nation," for that form of group life which was originally most revolutionary, and for its progress throughout historical development toward the modern national state, even though it consisted of those classes that overcame the obstacles to this evolution, the power of church, nobility, peasantry, feudal interests, hereditary principalities and their cadres of state officials. Not only the *proletariat,* in so far as it is internationally minded, but also entirely *new classes* have separated themselves from the bourgeoisie proper and have tended either to rise above it or to sink beneath it. The group that fell is the growing class of employees in large private enterprises which have continually become more bureaucratic; the group that rose represents the magnates of finance and the energizing industries. The independent middle classes which, in recent times, were the support of French national power politics (Poincaré), have, in all countries, been hit, more or less severely, by the war. All these *new* groups tend, however, more or less vigorously, to form *international* groups which cut *across* nations. This will forcibly bring about more and more tolerance for other countries, an attitude which resembles the tolerance for other confessions that resulted from the Thirty Years' War. When I visited the last convention of the League for Cultural Cooperation, founded by Prince Rohan, held in Heidelberg and Frankfurt, I was considerably surprised, in spite of my close acquaintance with this movement over several years, that the tendencies there expressed resembled so closely the spirit and policies of the "Holy Alliance." If they were somewhat less "holy," they were so much the more impelled by a growing fear, shared by the great bourgeois classes in Europe, that their power as a class would be endangered by any future war between nations. We can, in the future, count on the growth of pacifism in the capitalistic upper bourgeoisie. Europeanism, advanced by the lower as well as by the upper classes of society, is indeed our *destiny,* not our choice. And here again, it is our task to guide the adjustment politically and economically into the proper channels and forms.

Even the opposition between *capitalistic* and *socialistic* societies, which so exclusively preoccupies our epoch, will find its adjustment. Again we ask whether the political ability of future elites will suffice to effect it *peacefully* or whether it will come about not only through bloody class struggle but also through class wars. The difficult problems indicated by the two slogans have changed their meaning in two ways since the prewar period. The old, once essentially *internal,* problem of socialism versus capitalism is beginning to find a parallel of almost equal importance in the conflict between the national welfare state, concerned with the welfare of its total community, and the powerful commercial alliances which follow North American patterns and also work for international association. And it is even

more significant that, today, powerful states and entire national entities (England, Russia) like to see themselves identified with the
opposition between bourgeoisie and proletariat, whereas only class
distinction within a *single* state had previously existed. As a consequence, the imminent class struggle takes on the much more threaten-
ing and somber character of a class *war*. Thus, a problem of internal
politics has, increasingly, become one of foreign policy. There is no
darker cloud on the political horizon of Europe and, above all, in
Germany, than the tensions between London and Moscow. There is
no greater danger for our nation than that one or another power of
the European continent might let itself be engulfed in a power conflict between England and Russia, or that they might, by favoring
such a policy, encourage England, today still hesitant, to draw the
sword against Russia. The very *question* of how to act in such a
case, if put to our people, would drive a terrifying *wedge* into our
German nation and would cause something of a spiritual civil war.
Even the well-justified promise of our statesmen to maintain "strict
neutrality" can hardly save us in such a case, for the very maintenance
of neutrality demands power, and primarily military power. A weak
German state, in its particular geographic location, will hardly be
able to maintain this postulate of neutrality. If, however, the nations
of the continent remain united in every respect, at Geneva too, this
international adjustment between capitalistic and communistic orders
ran very well occur peacefully. Russia has had to adopt more and
more from capitalism since the Soviet republic and the new economic
order were established, and, even as a state, it regains more and more
of its typical *national* pattern with the rising predominance of the
peasantry. On the other hand, the so-called "capitalistic" nations, in
spite of maintaining the principle of private property, increasingly
absorb so much so-called socialism of all kinds, of fully or partially
collectivized economic policy, that the *actual conditions* on both sides
bridge more and more the contradictions between names and concepts.[8]

Whoever and wherever he may be, the person who works for

the new elite and for this adjustment between classes will have to encompass the different *kinds of thought, moral codes,* and *religious* modes of life which he finds in the upper and lower classes; he will have to reconcile them through an *inner* adjustment in spirit and heart. I have elsewhere developed this problem in detail, as it affects the different ideologies.[9] We are faced with two basic philosophies of history. The conception of the past as predominantly collective experience *or* as primarily the work of great personalities; history as dialectical process *or* as the sum of happenings within the "limits" of a stable, teleological "divine order"; praise of the "good old days" for fear of the future *or* eschatological hope and an enduring expectation of some utopian ideal which implies a stern rejection of the past; a rather materialistic *or* a rather ideological philosophy of history. *Neither* of the two philosophies results from the nature of things, but both are logical categories, *ideologies,* exclusively dependent on class myth. They testify that interests are more powerful than reason. Everyone who wants to see clearly in politics must abandon them *both.*

Therefore, only the person who knows how to take the sources of *deception* into account, the effect of his belonging to a class and of his participation in the *mythos* of national history, only the person who knows how to ban these webs from his mental eye can see realities with sober clarity and discern possible ways of bridging the contradictions they entail. For this reason, a thorough reform in the teaching of history is of highest importance. As long as "classical" ideology with its conception of man and history and the related, one-sided theism rules our upper classes, just that long will the lower classes, and the states which have risen to defend their interests, adhere to their naturalism which profanes the spirit and, reduced to a blunt formula, signifies, "man is what he eats," or will adhere to some similar but more refined ideology and mock all of man's metaphysical ties.

One should not delude oneself into thinking that the mass of the proletariat can ever be won back to any kind of organized religion or be recaptured by *any* kind of creed, even though the church, today, has gained in power through the confusion and despair of the bourgeoisie and through the consequent decrease in the authority of the state. The Christian idea of a purely spiritual, creative God, of the fall of man, and of the hereditary, irremediably sinful constitution of man, through which Christianity explains a great number of natural and social evils, such as war, the use of force by states, prostitution, etc., as if they were in some measure inevitable and not subject to reform—all these concepts, just like the classical idea of man with all its variants, are exclusively *ideologies of the upper class*. Furthermore, the fact that personalized theism had its ethnic origin exclusively in the great Eastern monarchies proves that it is a monarchic ideology with a strongly paternalistic culture and mentality. *Pantheistic* conceptions of God as "pure spirit" (Hegel) are also basically upper-class ideologies. The lower class will, as we have said, maintain its *purely* naturalistic conception of man, associated with an exclusively social and economic explanation of religion and of its authorities, as long as the upper class believes only in the *spontaneous* power of pure spirit, the active, positive force of pure will, and is not satisfied with a *"guiding and directing"* role of spiritual will in man and in human history, just as long as the upper class makes its belief into the basis for its political and social efforts, especially in the field of education.

A completely *metaphysical and religious* and, therefore, also political and social *integration and reconciliation of classes* will be possible only on the basis of a metaphysics, a conception of self, world, and God, which comprises light and darkness, the spirit and the fate-determining, demonic drive for existence and life. This conception roots man, both as a creature of *spirit* and of *drive*, in the divine source of all things; it accepts the general and total *dependence* of life or nature on spirit, along with the dependence of spirit on life and nature; and it integrates this interdependence into the idea of the source of the world which, as substance, stands above both poles of this contrast, and in which the *reconciliation of spirit and life,* of *idea and power,* takes place, although only in the course of world history and not independently of human action.

The sociology of religions and metaphysical systems, a field in which Max Weber, Ernst Troeltsch, Carl Schmitt, and some ethnologists have made very important contributions, has as its objective to relate the ideas of God and salvation to *social patterns* and forms of political rule.[10] It is not true, as Karl Marx thought, that the world of religious ideas can be derived directly from historical patterns or even from conditions of economic production. However, both are related by an inner bond, a common, ultimate conception and attitude toward being, as hard as it may be to recognize and identify. If this common bond does not exist, if the total life of man is no longer alive and permeated by inner religious perception, religion becomes a dead tradition. In such a case, it no longer unifies men, as does the true essence of all living conceptions of transcendental and holy values, but it separates and divides men. Only then does religion assume what Marx erroneously considered its ultimate nature, the expression of non-spiritual interests of all kinds and the expression of an ideology that wishes to render outdated social conditions permanent in order to benefit a certain class. Contemporary ideas of man and divinity, which can change only *simultaneously,* are indeed such that they *no longer correspond to the historical stage* of being, nor to the present social structure of mankind. They place man into a relationship to the source of the world characteristic of periods of immaturity, when humanity is staunchly segregated into separate cultural groups and has little impetus toward adjustment. This is why we must considerably revise our view of the metaphysical place of man in the cosmos and do our utmost to integrate it into historical reality.

Thus, we have indicated the metaphysical ideas within the limits of which the new elite, including the political elite, will move in its *relations to religion and metaphysics.* I would like to add a few comments about the fundamental attitude of the elite toward church *creeds.*

I believe that there are *four* possible attitudes of a political *elite* with respect to religion and metaphysics. The first is credal faith in church dogma with *all* its consequences, complete self-integration into the church, whether in simple faith or through wilful submission to church ethics and canon law. The second attitude is denoted by the words, *"écrasez l'infâme"* [crush the beast], e.g., the policy of the Soviet republic and of orthodox Marxism in general. The third attitude is that of Machiavelli, widely practiced today by the *Action française* and by Fascism. The politician himself is here a complete skeptic with respect to religion and operates on principles of power. Externally, he favors religion and the church as a means of taming the masses or as a "mythos of the nation," but, in reality, he is quite indifferent to it, if he does not despise it. The fourth attitude is that of *all* great ancient and modern philosophers toward organized religion and metaphysics, since Plato and Aristotle, via Spinoza to Goethe, Hegel, Schopenhauer, and Eduard von Hartmann. The keenest expression of this attitude was furnished by Spinoza: "Religion is the metaphysics of the masses, metaphysics the religion of thinkers." While the masses invoke and honor what is veiled by pictures and symbols, the thinker selects their pure and valid components and raises them reverently into the sphere of thought. A profound *identity of meaning* unites the two in their different approaches to the absolute, as long and in so far as both are involved in *living* movements of spirit.

As for the four attitudes, the second is completely senseless, since *some* kind of religious mythos belongs to the existence of every nation and since "the masses will never be philosophers" (Plato). The third position is a repulsive sham which falsely isolates the political element from the whole of man and brings with it the decomposition of religion and of the church itself. With respect to the first position, I must say this: It is most unlikely that an elite, today, can stand in such complete agreement with the doctrines of any organized church and, at the same time, do justice to the demands of the historical moment, without having to bend and twist these doctrines so much that only the *semblance* of agreement remains. Catholic circles, for instance, have seriously discussed whether the terms of the Weimar Constitution concerning the sovereignty of the German people are not in direct opposition to the strong condemnation of this principle by the highest church authority.

My conviction leads me to believe that the elite, as a group that must guide the coming adjustment into the right paths, may *not* give allegiance to *any* organized church. Such an elite will look reverently upon the great religious traditions and ecclesiastical institutions, fight to prevent confessional disputes, and demand free exchange of opinions, on the highest spiritual and moral plane, concerning the worth and truth of organized religion. It will not base its own metaphysical view of the ultimate as exclusively on the tradition of Luther, Kant, and German idealism, as the elites in the recent German past have done. Neither will it base itself exclusively on any other tradition, but will make room for the *fullness and variety of insight* which the history of religion and metaphysics offers. Essentially, the elite will derive its picture of God and world, to which its life and deed are committed, from the *spontaneous* forces of its own spirit, from its own experience in the world and history, observing the example and teaching of all great thinkers of the past. And from this firm position, it will, first of all, try to *decide* which elements of the established dogma of a church, of its idea of justice, and its ethics are or are not *relevant* to the conceptions acquired in its own debate with the fullness of reality. In doing so, it will keep in mind that, in the sphere of meaning and of spiritual values, pictorial symbols and historical accounts, which are characteristic of all organized religions, may, in many respects, coincide with rational views and conceptions and with specific moral philosophies. As Hegel very appropriately remarked, the same "meaning" may appear in the imagery of religious faith and in the form of a philosophic concept.

I will say nothing about the ultimate and highest object of adjustment in the coming era, adjustment between the content of our various metaphysical ideas of God, world, and man. Still, I venture to affirm that, even in this highest objective sphere, we can observe an increasing, almost strange, *convergence* of all fundamental opinions among the spiritual elites of thinkers in all nations, and that, here as well, an adjustment of tremendous proportions is in full progress although, so far, very few persons have apprehended it.

Notes

I PHILOSOPHER'S OUTLOOK

1. Cf. "Probleme einer Soziologie des Wissens," in Scheler, *Die Wissensformen und die Gesellschaft* (Leipzig, 1926), critical comments on historicism and positivism.

2. Cf. "Erkenntnis und Arbeit," in Scheler, *op. cit.*, p. 455 f on reality, p. 278 f on the idea of knowledge.

3. Cf. Scheler, *Die Stellung des Menschen im Kosmos* (1928) [(5th ed.; Munich, 1949), p. 26 f].

4. *Ibid.* [p. 65 f], and "Probleme einer Soziologie des Wissens," section I.

5. Further discussions of these issues: (i) Concerning the nature of philosophy: E. Husserl, "Philosophie als strenge Wissenschaft," *Logos* I (1910). Scheler, "Vom Wesen der Philosophie," *Vom Ewigen im Menschen* (1921) [4th ed.; Bern, 1954]; also, "The Forms of Knowledge and Culture" in this collection, Essay II. (ii) Concerning metaphysical knowledge: N. Hartmann, *Metaphysik der Erkenntnis.* Scheler, "Erkenntnis und Arbeit"; and "Idealismus-Realismus," *Philosophischer Anzeiger* II, 3 (Bonn, 1927). (iii) Concerning philosophical anthropology: Scheler, *Die Stellung des Menschen im Kosmos.* (iv) Concerning ethics: Scheler, *Der Formalismus in der Ethik und die materiale Wertethik* (1913-16) [4th ed.; Bern, 1954]. N. Hartmann, *Ethik* (Berlin, 1926). (v) Concerning the philosophy of nature: H. Weyl in *Handbuch der Philosophie* (Munich, 1927), fasc. 5. H. Driesch, *Philosophie des Organischen.* Cf. also the vols. of *Jahrbuch für Philosophie und phänomenologische Forschung* (Halle, 1913 sq.), ed. E. Husserl.

II THE FORMS OF KNOWLEDGE AND CULTURE

1. Cf. the measured, well-considered judgment of Rothenbucher, professor of canon law at Munich, in *Hochschulnachrichten* (1925).

2. What I have briefly indicated here is elaborated in "Probleme einer Soziologie des Wissens," in my book *Die Wissensformen und die Gesellschaft* (Leipzig, 1926) and in Ernst Troeltsch, "Die Revolution in der Wissenschaft," *Aufsätze zur Geistesgeschichte und Religionssoziologie* (Tübingen, 1924), II, 653.

3. More profound arguments for the idea of microcosm are given in my book *Der Formalismus in der Ethik und die materiale Wertethik* [(4th rev. ed.; Bern, 1954), p. 406 f]. Man, as a physical, as well as a psychic and noetic being, is an instance where all known *types* of principles are applied—mechanical, physical, chemical, sociological, psychological, and also noetic. Noetic principles

express the essence of rational spirit, therefore also of divine spirit, if it exists. Concerning the metaphysical import of the idea of microcosm, see the essay "Probleme der Religion" in my book *Vom Ewigen im Menschen.*

4. For what follows, cf. my essay, "Zur Idee des Menschen," in *Vom Umsturz der Werte.* H. Klaatsch, in his book *Werdegang der Menschheit,* was first to emphasize man's peculiarity in maintaining the most ancient evolutionary characteristics of land animals (e.g., the hand with five fingers) and in not adapting to the very specific conditions of his environment. Cf. also *Die Stellung des Menschen im Naturganzen* by the same author. Man is the true *dilettante* of life. This refusal to adapt also conditions his attempt to adapt nature to himself rather than adjusting to it. Recently, Edgar Dacqué, in his book *Urwald, Sage und Menschheit,* goes still further with the idea that man is a conservative species. He does this in the scientifically sound *parts* of his book. A similar attitude, from a physiological point of view, is adopted by Ehrenberg in *Theoretische Biologie* (Berlin, 1924). In my *Philosophische Anthropologie,* I shall examine the philosophic implications of the origin of man as seen by natural history, the modern problems brought up by Klaatsch, Schwalbe, Steinmann, and Dacqué, and I shall relate these questions to man's psychological evolution and metaphysical problems. [*Philosophische Anthropologie* was not published by the author; cf. instead *Die Stellung des Menschen im Kosmos.*]

5. Cf. my psychophysical theory in *Philosophische Anthropologie.* The elements which one can establish only in the abstract (value and feeling, picture and imagination, quality and sensation, significance of an object and concept, force and trend, and desire and drive, etc.) as well as the categories of principles (e.g., formal mechanistic principles, teleoclinic principles relating to a whole) are common to the external and inner worlds. According to my theory, there is no so-called causal "reciprocal effect" between the forces of these two worlds, but only a (guiding and directing) *effectiveness* or *non*-effectiveness of the inner spiritual centers on the external psychophysiological sequence of events and, furthermore, of the inner life center (psychophysically neutral, the center of a bundle of functions with individual differences and structure but pertaining to *one* universal life) on external events of a formal, mechanistic character. Only the principles of spiritual-noetic acts find *no* parallel in physiology. Theirs is a *constant principle,* a category of being, pertaining to being itself, such as philosophical ontology investigates.

6. A. von Tschermak, *Allgemeine Physiologie,* Vol. I, and Ehrenberg, *Theoretische Biologie,* discuss whether we can arrive at a conception according to which vital functions create structural patterns, and what difficulties remain to be solved.

7. To document these statements see also: Rubner, *Kraft und Stoff im Haushalte der Nature* (Leipzig, 1909), Friedenthal, *Allgemeine und spezielle Physiologie des Menschenwachstums* (Berlin, 1914), Ehrenberg, *Theoretische Biologie* (Berlin, 1924). Cf. further the investigations of L. Edinger of the functions of the cerebral cortex in man and dog, also "Der Mensch ohne Grosshirn," *Archiv für die gesammte Physiologie,* Vol. 152; F. R. Goltz, "Der Hund ohne Grosshirn," *ibid.* Vol. 51; and M. Rothmann, "Der Hund ohne Grosshirn," *Neur. Zentralblatt,* Vol. 28. The case of a child without cerebrum, investigated by Edinger, shows that the powers remaining to the child were *far smaller* than those of a dog without cerebrum.

8. Cf. Ehrenberg, *Theoretische Biologie;* pertinent comment also in W. Stern, *Person und Sache,* Vol. I. In my *Philosophische Anthropologie,* I try to develop a detailed philosophical theory of old age and death which deals with physiological and psychic aspects and also with the death of the individual and the species.

9. If we were to consider the values of biological life the *highest,* we would logically have to accept consequences which I have examined in detail in my book *Der Formalismus in der Ethik und die materiale Wertethik* [(4th ed.; Bern, 1954), pp. 289-309]. Actually, all human spiritual aspirations which ever existed are based on the assumption that biological life is *not* the highest of values. Neither the values of ethics nor those of knowledge or esthetics can be biologically justified, nor can we derive value *judgments* from biology or vitalistic psychology (as Spencer, Nietzsche, J. M. Guyau, and others believed). The study of the theory of value proves the *autonomy of the spirit* in man, no less clearly than logic, the theory of knowledge, and ontology, and does so quite independently from these disciplines. Concerning "conscience," cf. the excellent study by H. Stoker, "Das Gewissen" (Bonn, 1925), in *Schriften zur Philosophie und Soziologie,* edited by myself. Kant said quite correctly: "If nature's real aim for a creature endowed with reason and will were its maintenance and well-being, in short, its happiness, nature made poor provision in choosing the reason of this creature as the agent of its intent. All actions which man must undertake to achieve this objective, happiness, and the general rule of his behavior could be derived far more accurately from *instinct.* Instinct could have realized all his goals far more surely than reason ever can" *(Grundlegung der Metaphysik der Sitten,* section 1).

10. In proposing this, I am following my dynamic theory of matter which, for years, I have been presenting in my lectures as closely related to my theory of space and time. The commentary of Eduard von Hartmann (see his *Kategorienlehre*) still seems the best philosophical treatment of the problem. Weyl recently embarked on an interesting attempt to explain the dynamic theory of matter from the standpoint of mathematical physics. See his work *Was ist Materie?* (Berlin, 1925). Cf. also "Erkenntnis und Arbeit" in my book *Die Wissensformen und die Gesellschaft* (Leipzig, 1926).

11. We explain man as a "spiritual living being," a "microcosm," a creature capable of "guiding" and "directing," i.e., of controlling and releasing his drives and conceptions (the ascetic of life) according to principles of action which are, *simultaneously,* constant ontological principles. I wish to point out that this *idea of the essence of man* leaves *complete freedom* for all possible categories of anatomy, physiology, and vitalistic psychology. The idea is strictly *formal* and refers to pure aspects of being which lack all empirical characteristics, i.e., those based on observation and induction. Man on earth, as he might be distinguished from men living on other heavenly bodies of different chemical and physical constitution and composition, is only a special case as compared with the *idea* of man. This is particularly true for the evolutionary stages of man which we must assume between *Pithecanthropus erectus* (Dubois) and *homo sapiens* (Heidelberg man, *Eoanthropus,* Neanderthal man, etc.). Edgar Dacqué proposed a very remarkable theory of biological *structural styles* of life in different periods ("characteristics of periods"). It lets man go back to the very origin of land animals and assumes

radically different forms in man's physical and psychological make-up (see the summary diagram, p. 252 of his book) between "original, amphibious, horn-coated man walking on all fours" and the man of the ice age whom we know through fossils. The assumptions of our own idea of the essence of man would be valid even if Edgar Dacqué were right, just as our *idea of the unity* of man and of his true *essence* is not contradicted by the ever more probable theory of polygenesis, to explain the natural origins of man and human races. I agree that the inductive empirical concepts of man must be viewed as completely *relative*. There is *no* "uniform nature of man" in an empirical-psychological, biologic and historical sense. Our "idea" of man admits this unlimited relativity of man as a concept of natural science and psychology, and we consider this a special *advantage* of our idea. W. Roux has shown that we must understand the concept of a *living being* (probably to include animals and plants) in the context of ontological phenomenology (if only because of the established fact that there is *no* physico-chemical definition of life). Recently, Tschermak did likewise in the excellent introduction to his *Allgemeine Psychologie*, Vol. I. Cf. the often profound remarks on the application of this theory to plants and animals by the botanist Hans André, *Der Wesensunterschied von Pflanze, Tier und Mensch* (Habelschwerdt, 1925).

12. In recent years, Wolfgang Köhler has done most for animal psychology in Germany. His studies of chimpanzees are well known. The important second (theoretical) volume of the work has not yet appeared. An extensive literature, we need not cite here, is based on Köhler's theory of the way chimpanzees gain "insight." Recently, Friedrich Alverdes, in his book *Neue Bahnen in der Lehre vom Verhalten der niederem Organismen* (Berlin, 1922), has clearly shown that the principle of practice movements and "trial and error" is quite insufficient for understanding even the *lower* organisms. Concerning the problems of the origin of language, cf. the excellent summary of findings by Delacroix, *Le langage et la pensée* (Paris, 1924), also my essay "Zur Idee des Menschen."

13. In my *Philosophische Anthropologie,* I shall justify in detail the proposition that all specific achievements of man, and the complex functions underlying them, can be derived from the three essential conditions of man.

14. Leibnitz said appropriately, in his *Monadology* (section 29): "The knowledge of eternal and necessary truths distinguishes us from mere animals and equips us with reason and sciences, by uplifting us to perceive ourselves and God."

15. The assumption of the basically negative nature of the spiritual "will" (in so far as the will is related to action rather than to the appraisal of an ideal project), which is superior to drives and which controls and releases impulses, is also fundamental for pedagogy. In our metaphysics, this assumption is also applicable to the wilful element in the spirit of the *one* divine, real source of the world which contains the two attributes we know, "spirit" and "drive." We do not derive the origin of the world from a "creation out of nothing," as does theism, but from the *"non non fiat"* [it shall not be non-existent], through which the divine spirit released the demonic drive in order to realize the idea of the divine which had been only a "potential." In order to realize "himself," God *had to accept in exchange* the substance of the

world and world history. By "free will" we understand only the act which corresponds to existence, or to realizing the project, not its *content*, i.e., not the circumstance of the project motivated by strict *necessity*, experience, inherited and vital psyche, nor the *particular* essence of the person which transcends time. Man, endowed with free will, can, therefore, be called the *"negator," the "ascetic of life."* Thus, in all cases, the spirit is not a creative principle, but only one which sets limits, maintains fortuitous reality within the *bounds* of possible being. Cf. also my "Probleme der Soziologie des Wissens," section I, where I discuss the role of the spirit in *history* as it faces the "factors of reality."

16. The great German mystics, Master Ekkehart in particular, assumed this kind of *solidarity* and interplay between the timeless *growing being of divinity* and *world history,* or, better, the world *as* history, especially the origin and history of man in which the essence of all other things on earth is represented in microcosm. Cf. H. Heimsoeth, *Die sechs Hauptthemen der abendländischen Metaphysik* (Berlin, 1922), chapter "Gott und Welt."

Among the philosophers of the nineteenth century, this idea was first strongly stated by Hegel's *Phänomenologie des Geistes,* in the famous words: "The life of God and divine perception may be regarded as a play of love with itself, but this idea is depreciated into cheap edification and insipidness if it lacks earnestness, pain, patience, and an active negative principle" (Preface).

Eduard von Hartmann has taken up the same idea in a one-sided manner, on the basis of his metaphysical pessimism ("all existence is evil as such"). According to him, man liberated the divinity from its blind power to act which had determined the existence of the world. Thus Hartmann combined Schopenhauer's idea that salvation follows from the "negation of will" with Hegel's idea of world development and progress. Our own metaphysical belief is this: *The realization of spirit* in divine substance which always posits itself through the second known attribute of divinity, *drive,* and *the ideation of drive* ("spiritualization of life") are both the *same,* metaphysically *identical* process, once seen from the standpoint of "spirit" and "essence," the other time from "drive" and "existence." World history is, for us, the concrete, temporal manifestation of the fact that the fundamental opposition between spirit and drive (*natura naturans*) is resolved in the functional unity of the source of the world. Therefore, history is for us, also, *interpenetration* of spirit and power. The omniscient, infinitely good, *and* almighty God of theism stands, as we see it, at the end of the growth of divinity, not at the beginning of world evolution. It represents an ideal *objective* which is attained only in as far as the world (for us a *growing* organism, not a mechanism) *becomes* the perfect *body* of God. The theistic concept of God falsely attributes power to the spirit itself, even power to create, and inadequately explains evil and good only through the myth of fallen angels. In opposition, we testify with Walter Rathenau: 'Un dieu tout-puissant, tout-savant, parfait et calme, serait un ogre. Dieu souffre. Il s'efforce. Il aime. Il a pitié" [An all-powerful, omniscient, perfect, and calm divinity would be a monster. God suffers, strives, loves, pities] (*Aus Walter Rathenaus Notizbüchern*). We have applied this metaphysical theory concerning the source of the world to explain history; see the first part of our "Probleme einer Soziologie des Wissens." Even such a sober scholar as Carl Stumpf, very skeptical in the face of metaphysical problems, believes: "The fact that God suffers and fights in us and with us may well be the most effective consolation for many of us." *Die Philosophie der Gegenwart in Selbstdarstellung* (Leipzig, 1924), V, 52.

17. The Renaissance was eminently significant because it *clearly and distinctly stood for* the intrinsic value of the *culture* of the whole man, not only theoretically, but by the active example of its great scholars, artists, and universal men. It stood in opposition to the medieval subordination of man to the church community and to its *"works,"* also in complete opposition to the *idea of professional specialization* held by Protestants of all kinds. In the essay "Renaissance and Reformation" (1913), E. Troeltsch compares the Protestant affirmation of the world, taken as an affirmation of professional specialization, with the affirmation of the world by the Renaissance. He judges very correctly: "How very different is the affirmation of the world of the Renaissance! It is in no way tied to the idea of professional specialization which, for Protestantism, has become the synthesis of the world and of ascetic life. Indeed, the Renaissance does not even know the concept of specialization. On the contrary, it can be identified with free artistic education, free scholarly research, self-representation, and individual culture, and with their emancipation from all fetters of bourgeois patterns of specialization. . . . Its aim is the *uomo universale,* the *galantuomo* [universal man, gentleman], the man dedicated to intellectual freedom and culture, the very opposite of the professional man and specialist" (*Aufsätze zur Geistesgeschichte und Religionssoziologie* [1924], I, 281). The fault of the cultural ideal of the Renaissance was, however, what we criticize in our text, the individualistic idea of *culture for its own sake.* This aspect, not a preference given to culture over specialized education, places the Renaissance ideal in sharp *opposition* to the idea of professional training. Concerning the extremely one-sided predominance of professional specialization over the idea of culture in Germany since Bismarck, and for its consequences, see my book *Die Ursachen des Deutschenhasses,* 2nd ed. This is one instance where the fruits of the Renaissance were lost in Germany because of the Reformation.

18. I have thoroughly proved these important statements in my book *Der Formalismus in der Ethik und die materiale Wertethik* [(4th ed.; Bern, 1954), p. 113 f].

19. First principle: In its *fortuitous existence,* the spirit of man is not an absolute substance, as the older theories concerning the substantial nature of the soul used to propose, but it is a self-concentration of the *one* divine spirit, as *one* of the knowable attributes of the source of the world. The unity of the spiritual "person" is only the unity of a concrete center of acts, a functional, structural unity, *organized* in accordance with the fundamental principles of the acts. Its culmination (the most valued degree of preference) may be taken up by *different* acts. It is *not* a unity of substance, such as we see in the source of the world, and is, therefore, not a "creature." Second principle: In its particular nature, the spiritual person in man is individualized, not in body and heredity, nor in experience derived through the medium of psychic vital functions, but *through itself and in itself.* For this reason alone, spiritual persons, in no way individualized, or, rather, in no way singled out by their position in space and time, can *have a multiple aspect.* The first of

these principles was recognized by Spinoza, who was unaware of the second; the second was known to Duns Scotus and Suarez without awareness of the first. Cf. *ibid.* [p. 381 f]; also *Wesen und Formen der Sympathie* [(5th ed.; Frankfurt, 1949), p. 134 f].

20. All general conclusions in the form "all A is B," if they do not follow from essential relationships, have only the negative meaning "if there is no A, B is not present." This is an important logical insight of Franz Brentano. The laws of nature are certainly *not essential* relationships but, as Leibnitz stated, entirely "contingent." E. Mach calls them, with an unfortunate subjective connotation, "restrictions of our expectations," and thereby correctly notes their negative character. Physicists are asking themselves at present whether, aside from the laws of nature of the statistical type, of the "greatest number," such as many laws of thermodynamics, there might also be dynamic and "necessary" laws of nature. Planck thinks so; Nernst does not. Their differences could be resolved by assuming that all kinds of law, which do not concern *purely* essential relationships, have *only* statistical significance. Even the principle of the conservation of energy was recently found to be merely statistical. In the theory of knowledge, the assumption of law in nature is only a *vitalistic* a priori of choice, not a rational a priori which is ontologically valid. All moral laws of behavior, related to a purely objective idea of good and evil, have only the significance of statistical averages, as recently, an Englishman, G. E. Moore, has perfectly demonstrated in his book *Ethics* (London: Home University Library). The purely *negative* significance of these laws, related to the idea, "the a priori good for myself," is discussed in detail in my *Ethics* [Cf. *Der Formalismus* (4th ed., Bern, 1954), pp. 337 f, 494 f, 512 f]. Cf. also the essay of G. Simmel, "Das individuelle Gesetz," in his last book *Lebensanschauung. Vier metaphysische Kapitel* (Munich, 1918).

21. See "Probleme einer Soziologie des Wissens," in my book *Die Wissensformen und die Gesellschaft* (Leipzig, 1926).

22. Cf. A. Meinong, *Über Möglichkeit und Wahrscheinlichkeit* (Leipzig, 1915).

23. The wide variety of ways in which modern philosophers explain the nature of knowledge is due to the *basic* fact that they undertake to determine the general nature of knowledge from the standpoint of individual sciences and their particular methods (mathematics, physics, history, etc.). There is equal confusion in defining the *kinds of knowledge* (experimental-scientific, metaphysical) and the basic operations subservient to knowledge, e.g., acquaintance with facts (information), perception, recognition, explanation, grasp, comprehension, and, finally, perception coupled with thought, e.g., judgment. At least three quarters of our theorists of knowledge say, for instance, that knowledge is judgment. This *cannot be,* since a judgment can be true or false, and since it is evidently *nonsensical* to speak of "false knowledge." Knowledge can be evident or non-evident, adequate or inadequate, relative or absolute, but *never* true or false. The theory of a *system of standards of knowledge* (among which the measure true-false is but *one* of many) is still in its infancy. The definitions of knowledge, cited above, are all false or one-sided, based on incomplete criteria applicable to certain kinds of knowledge. My theory of knowledge, which I have for years presented in my lectures, has not yet been published

in systematic form, a circumstance most unfortunate for the understanding of my philosophy. I shall publish it in Volume I of my *Metaphysik*. It will also contain a critical discussion of the theories of knowledge held by the various schools outlined above. [Cf. "Erkenntnis und Arbeit" (1926), p. 245 f].

24. For seven years I have been proposing the following ideas in my lectures, as a *basis* for my theory of knowledge. Consciousness (a translation of *con-scientia*) is only one form of knowledge. There also exists preconscious, ecstatic knowledge (therefore, knowledge is, in no way, a function of "consciousness"). Knowledge itself is, however, an *ontological* relationship. The circumstantial presence of what is can simultaneously be *in mente* and *extra mentem,* but existence is always *extra mentem.* Furthermore, the fact that we possess existence as such is *not* at all based on intellectual factors (whether perception or thought), but solely on the *resistance* of what is, originally experienced only in the act of striving and in the dynamic factors of attention. Nicolai Hartmann, in his recent book *Metaphysik der Erkenntnis,* also derived knowledge from an ontological relationship, of course, without a "will-directed" theory of existence, which alone can give this derivation its full significance. Therefore, this profound author soon falls back on an explanation of knowledge as "representation" of extra-mental objects. Thus he returns to "critical realism." We sharply reject this school along with any idealism of consciousness. While idealism of consciousness clearly and correctly sees, as critical realism does not, that the circumstantial presence of things must be *in mente,* it falsely believes that existence can also be *in mente.* While critical realism sees correctly that existence, always and necessarily, is *extra mentem,* it wrongly believes that the circumstantial presence of things can be *extra mentem* and only *extra mentem,* i.e., that it can only be an image (a representation) or a symbol of the circumstantial presence of things *in mente.* The false assumption common to both theories is this: They believe that the existence and the circumstance of things, as related to the intellect (perception, thought, memory) are *inseparable* from each other. [Cf. Max Scheler, "Idealismus-Realismus," *Philos. Anzeiger,* II (Bonn, 1927), 3; also the essay "Erkenntnis und Arbeit."]

25. This is true because the existence of things (which idealism usually confuses with the concreteness of what exists) belongs directly only to the realm of drives and will, as what is effectively resisting us. It does not pertain to any of the forms of "knowledge." Ontologically as well, it lies in the nature of existence *never* to be a necessary consequence of the Logos, but to be *dynamically posited.* (Schelling and Eduard von Hartmann have clearly recognized this). Only when we ask—does what pertains to circumstance also possess existence?—is it *something* that has the character of reality, only then does the relationship of laws, into which this something is organized, become the decisive factor. These relationships are completely different in essence for what is inanimate and for what is animate and spiritual, but they are *identical* in kind for biological and psychological factors. It is completely erroneous to state (as do the Neo-Kantians): "Existence" and "reality" *designate* only the organization into "relationships of laws," and, furthermore, relationships of laws are always of the same kind, i.e., formal and mechanical.

26. The hierarchy of the three objectives of the growth of knowledge exactly corresponds to the hierarchy of the modalities of value (value of sanctity, spirit, and fortuitous existence) which I developed and carefully proved in my

Ethics (see: *Der Formalismus in der Ethik* [(4th ed.; Bern, 1954), p. 125 f]).
We are not simply re-creating, in the divine spirit, the *"ideae ante res"* [ideas,
forms anterior to world reality] which were present even before the world became
reality. The differentiation of ideas out of the Λόγος (a component of the first
attribute of the source of the world, the divine "spirit") is accomplished only
under the purposeful impulsion of the creative *drive* (second attribute) which
originally had been blind. The differentiation began when this drive became
effective in positing existence. Therefore, the source of the world itself "learns"
(in a way) from the world process. We hope to prove this in detail in our
Metaphysik. Much excellent comment on this point can be found in the *Kategorienlehre* of Eduard von Hartmann; cf. the category of "substance" in the
metaphysical realm. We get a conception of the relationship between the source
of the world and the world as *creatio continua* (of bodies, centers of force and
vitalistic nature, also of nuclei of the spiritual person) which *excludes* the
theistic distinction between the creation and the conservation of the world.

27. Concerning this paragraph, cf. my essay "Probleme einer Soziologie des
Wissens," in my book *Die Wissensformen und die Gesellschaft* (Leipzig, 1926)
[also "Erkenntnis und Arbeit," *ibid*.]; furthermore, my essay "Über die positivistische Geschichtsphilosophie des Wissens" (the principle of the three stages
in Auguste Comte), in *Schriften zur Soziologie und Weltanschauungslehre,*
Part I, *Moralia.*

28. Cf. my essay "Vom Wesen der Philosophie," in my book *Vom Ewigen
im Menschen* [4th ed.; Bern, 1954]; also, "Probleme einer Soziologie des
Wissens." Cf. further, H. Bäcker's profound analysis, *Der Ursprung des Kausal-
gedankens. Eine phänomenologische Studie über die Verwunderung* (diss.
Cologne, 1925).

29. Cf. my two essays, "Probleme einer Soziologie des Wissens" and
"Erkenntnis und Arbeit," in my book *Die Wissensformen und die Gesellschaft.*
In Vol. I of my *Metaphysik* [cf. "Idealismus-Realismus," *op. cit.*, Pt. II, Sec. 8,
and *Die Stellung des Menschen im Kosmos*] I shall outline in detail the theory
and technique of excluding the moment of reality and determine, in the case of
such an exclusion, the order in which specific objects of our image of the world
disappear so that we can conceive of "pure essence."

III *SPINOZA*

1. For his biography, cf. J. Freudenthal, *Spinoza, sein Leben und seine
Lehre* (Stuttgart, 1904).

2. Appendix to *Principia philosophiae,* a work of Spinoza concerning the
philosophy of Descartes.

3. Edited by Christoph Sigwart under the title, *Benedict de Spinozas
kurzer Tractat von Gott, dem Menschen und dessen Glückseligkeit* (Tübingen,
1870).

4. For the historical significance of the political theory and philosophy of
Spinoza, see Friedrich Meinecke, *Die Idee der Staatsraison* (Munich, 1924), p.
270 f.

5. Expertly edited by K. Gebhardt in the "Philosophische Bibliothek" of F. Meiner.

6. Cf. the important contribution of Carl Stumpf, "Spinoza Studien," in *Abhandlungen der Preussischen Akademie der Wissenschaften.*

IV *MAN AND HISTORY*

1. Cf. the remarkable comments on this mythos in E. Cassirer, *Philosophie der symbolischen Formen,* Vol. II.

2. Cf. the discourse on Spinoza in this collection of essays.

3. Cf. *Die Stellung des Menschen im Kosmos* [(5th ed.; Munich, 1949)], a short résumé of how the author views some of the cardinal issues of "philosophical anthropology." Over the years, the author has many times dealt with this field in his lectures, and in far greater detail than in the present sketch of essentials.

4. See the essay, "Zur Idee des Menschen" (1918), in the collection of essays entitled *Vom Umsturz der Werte* (3rd ed.; Leipzig, 1923).

5. Cf. the essay by Dilthey, "Erfahren und Denken" (1892), in *Gesammelte Schriften* (Leipzig, 1924), V, 88.

6. Cf. "Zur Idee des Menschen"; also the essay "Erkenntnis und Arbeit" in *Die Wissensformen und die Gesellschaft* (Leipzig, 1926), where the problem of pragmatism is discussed at length.

7. Cf. *Die Stellung des Menschen im Kosmos* [p. 33 f].

8. In his significant essay entitled *Jenseits des Lustprinzips,* p. 40, Sigmund Freud clearly enunciates *his* idea of man: "It may be hard for many of us to give up the belief that there dwells in man the drive to perfect himself, a drive which has brought him to his present high level of intellectual accomplishment and ethical sublimation and which can be expected to bring about his development into superman. I cannot believe in such an inner drive and see no way of salvaging this agreeable illusion. The past development of man seems, in my opinion, to require no other explanation than that of animals. The restless drive to achieve further perfection, which one can observe in a small minority of individuals, can easily be explained as a consequence of the *repression of drives,* on which the most valuable parts of human culture are based. — The processes which accompany the formation of a neurotic phobia, which is only an attempt to escape the satisfaction of drives, gives us an example of the origin of this supposed drive toward perfection. . . ."

9. Cf. the section, "Zur Philosophie der Wahrnehmung," in the essay, "Erkenntnis und Arbeit"; also, *Die Stellung des Menschen im Kosmos* [p. 71 f].

10. Cf. the essay, "Über die positivistische Geschichtsphilosophie des Wissens," in *Moralia,* in *Schriften zur Soziologie und Weltanschauungslehre, I* (Leipzig, 1923).

11. Cf. the excellent short contribution of H. Cysarz, *Literaturgeschichte als Geisteswissenschaft* (Halle, 1926).

12. Cf. L. Bolk, *Das Problem der Menschwerdung* (Jena, 1926).

13. Cf. P. Alsberg, *Das Menschheitsrätsel* (Dresden, 1922).

14. Concerning this and what follows, see *Die Stellung des Menschen im Kosmos* [p. 58 f].

15. Cf. "Probleme einer Soziologie des Wissens," in *Die Wissensformen und die Gesellschaft,* p. 78.

16. Concerning the relationship between the factors of ideation and realization, see Part I of the essay, "Zur Soziologie des Wissens"; also, *Die Stellung des Menschen im Kosmos* [p. 65 f].

17. See C. A. Bernoullis, *Bachofen und das Natursymbol* (Basle, 1924), very interesting as a cultural document; also A. Baeumler's introduction to his new edition of the major writings of Bachofen, in *Der Mythus von Orient und Okzident* (Munich, 1926). Further, Baeumler's contribution, *Bachofen und Nietzsche* (Zurich, 1929).

18. See L. Klages, *Mensch und Erde; Vom Wesen des Bewusstseins; Vom kosmogonischen Eros.* E. Dacqué, *Urwelt, Sage und Menschheit; Natur und Seele.* L. Frobenius, *Paideuma.* T. Lessing, *Der Untergang der Erde am Geist.*

19. Cf. also O. Spengler, *Der Untergang des Abendlandes,* Vol. II, last pages, where "spirit and money" definitely seem to be deprecated and where each nation that believes more in "truth and justice" than in increasing its power is expected to collapse.

20. In principle, this author, also, attributes such a function to the emotional drives. Cf. *Wesen und Formen der Sympathie* [(5th ed.; Frankfurt am Main, 1949)].

21. Cf. D. H. Kerler, *Weltwille und Wertwille* (Leipzig, 1926), also the short contribution, *Max Scheler und die impersonalistische Lebensanschauung* (Ulm, 1917). Furthermore, N. Hartmann, *Ethik* (Berlin and Leipzig, 1926), which, in many respects and most fruitfully, continues my efforts to establish a system of the ethics of material values.

22. Cf. K. Breysig, *Vom geschichtlichen Werden* (Stuttgart and Berlin, 1925-26).

V MAN IN THE ERA OF ADJUSTMENT

1. Cf. the comments on the dynamics of knowledge in "Probleme einer Soziologie des Wissens," in the book *Die Wissensformen und die Gesellschaft* (1926), p. 25 f.

2. Cf. "Das Nationale im Denken Frankreichs," in *Nation und Weltanschauung: Schriften zur Soziologie und Weltanschauungslehre II* (Leipzig, 1923).

3. Cf. "Probleme einer Soziologie des Wissens," pp. 63, 125.

4. Cf. *Die Stellung des Menschen im Kosmos* [(5th ed.; Munich, 1949)]; also, "Man and History" in this collection.

5. Here and for what follows, cf. the essay "Vom Sinn des Leidens," in *Moralia: Schriften zur Soziologie und Weltanschauungslehre I* (1922).

6. Cf. "The Forms of Knowledge and Culture" in this collection.

7. Cf. my fundamental explanations in "Universität und Volkshochschulen," in *Die Wissensformen und die Gesellschaft.*

8. I am here in complete agreement with the conclusions of W. Sombart,

concerning the "Zukunft des Kapitalismus," in *Der moderne Kapitalismus,* Vol. II, p. 1016.

9. Cf. "Probleme einer Soziologie des Wissens," p. 203 f.

10. I have made several comments concerning this point in my essay "Probleme einer Soziologie des Wissens."

Index

Absolute, knowledge of, 3
Achievement, knowledge of, 3-5
Acosmic pantheism, 53, 54
Action, metaphysics of, 11
Adjustment, 102; between principles, 111; European-Asiatic, 112; mental-physical, 117; political-economic, 118; capitalistic-socialistic, 119
Adler, Alfred, and *homo faber,* 78; and power politics, 80
Alexandrine-Hellenistic age, 17-18
Alsberg, Paul, on man, 83
Anaxagoras, on *homo sapiens,* 71
Animals, psychic qualities, 26; soul of, 27
Anthropology, philosophical, 9-10; and relationship with history, 68-69
Apollonian man, 87, 106
Aquinas, Thomas, on soul, 20; on man's metaphysical rank, 67; on theory of man, 73
Areopagita, Dionysius, 54
Aristotle, 1; first philosophy, 5; on love, 20; on philosophy, 44; and *homo sapiens,* 71; on theory of man, 73; on man's mind, 84; on existence, 117; on religion and metaphysics, 124
Asiatic cultures, 43
Atheism, 90-93
Atheistic pantheism, 53-54
Augustin, on concepts of history, 70
Avenarius, Richard, 2
Averroes, pantheism of, 50; and human and divine spirit, 68

Bachofen, on man, 87
Bacon, Francis, and *homo faber,* 78
Barrès, Maurice, 15

Bergson, Henri, on perception, 39; on man's losses, 87
Bible, a forbidden book, 14
Biology, and transformation of man, 71
Bismarck, von, Otto, on power politics, 81; on concept of God, 111
Blood, purifying, philosophy of, 80
Böhme, Jacob, 51
Bolk, Louis, on man, 83
Books, prohibited list, 14
Bossuet, Jacques B., on conceptions of history, 70
Bonn, Moritz Julius, 108
Breysig, Kurt, on historiography, 93
Bruno, Giordano, 51; on soul, 20; on love, 20; and renaissance pantheism, 54, 56; and concept of heaven, 67
Burgh, Albert, questions Spinoza's philosophy, 52-53

Capitalism, 100; and adjustment to socialism, 119
Carlyle, Thomas, on anthropology and history, 93
China, culture in, 48; European adjustment to, 112
Christianity, Spinoza on, 52; and concept of man, 69-71
City of God, 70
Civilizations, and man's consciousness of self, 66
Comte, Auguste, and *homo faber,* 78, 89; concept of history, 81; on atheism, 92
Concepts, of time and space, 4; of reality, 5
Control, knowledge of, 3-5; and drive, 5
Culture, knowledge of, 3, 5-9; and democracy, rise of, 16; Greek-

139

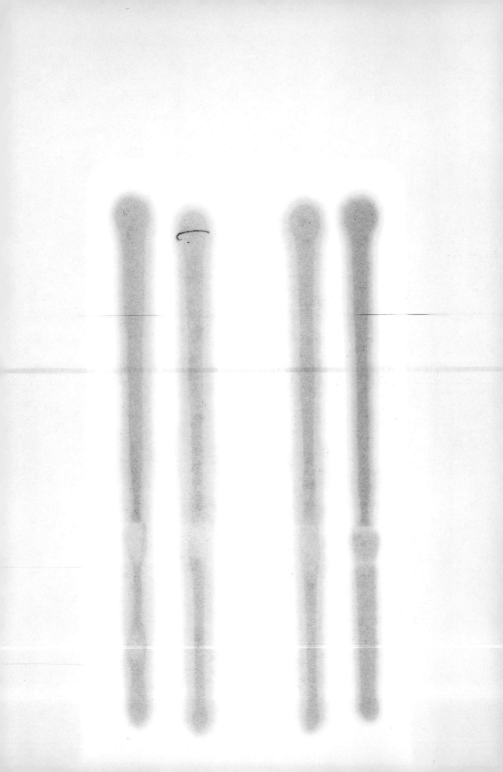